CAPTURING ZUMA – A CARTOONIST'S TALE

Zapiro

with Mike Wills

ACKNOWLEDGEMENTS

Thanks to Mike Wills and Marius Roux for another wonderful collaboration; the many editors at *Mail & Guardian*, *Sowetan*, *Sunday Times*, *Independent Newspapers* and *Daily Maverick* who've published my hard-hitting cartoons and backed me against Zuma's law suits; legal guru Dario Milo and the team at Webber Wentzel; Bro Russell at Cartoonists' Rights Network International and global cartoonists who drew in support; SA cartoonists who did the same; John Curtis and his Africartoons archive; my web manager Richard Hainebach and figurine sculptor Judd Simantov; Bridget Impey, Nadia Goetham and all at Jacana; my ever-adept assistant Eleanora Bresler; at home, Nomalizo Ndlazi and my family Karina, Tevya and Nina for their love and support through it all; the many readers who send ideas and let their light-bulb moments become mine; and finally, thanks to Jacob Zuma without whom none of this would have been possible, heh heh heh!

MORE BOOKS BY ZAPIRO

ZAPIRO annuals
The Madiba Years (1996)
The Hole Truth (1997)
End of Part One (1998)
Call Mr Delivery (1999)
The Devil Made Me Do It! (2000)
The ANC Went in 4x4 (2001)
Bushwhacked (2002)
Dr Do-Little and the African Potato (2003)
Long Walk to Free Time (2004)
Is There a Spin Doctor In the House? (2005)
Da Zuma Code (2006)
Take Two Veg and Call Me In the Morning (2007)
Pirates of Polokwane (2008)
Don't Mess With the President's Head (2009)
Do You Know Who I Am?! (2010)
The Last Sushi (2011)
But Will It Stand Up In Court? (2012)
My Big Fat Gupta Wedding (2013)
It's Code Red! (2014)
Rhodes Rage (2015)
Dead President Walking (2016)
Hasta la Gupta, baby! (2017)

Other books
The Mandela Files (2008)
VuvuzelaNation (2013)
DemoCrazy (2014)

First published by Jacana Media 2018

10 Orange Street
Sunnyside
Auckland Park 2092
South Africa
+27 11 628 3200

In association with

© Jonathan Shapiro, 2018
Text © Mike Wills, 2018

ISBN 978-1-4314-2713-0

Cover design by Zapiro and MR Design
Page layout by MR Design

Cartoon colouring by Roberto, pages 9, 18, 93, 96, 97, 99, 112, 140, 189, 219. The rest by Zapiro.

Figurines by Zapiro Collectibles, page 16
Social Media posts, pages 15, 195

Permission to publish cartoons:
page 13 Steve Bell; page 74 Madam & Eve (Rico and Stephen Francis), Chip Snaddon, Tony Grogan, Brandan Reynolds, Jeremy Nel; page 75 Damien Glez, Luis Eduardo Leon, Carlos Brito, José Maria 'Ché' Varona, Gado (Godfrey Mwampembwa)

Big Issue cover, Mikateko Media and The Big Issue, page 248

Photographs, page 6 and cover flap, Karina Turok.

Printed and bound by ABC Press, Cape Town
Job no. 003333

See a complete list of Jacana titles at www.jacana.co.za

CONTENTS

- 4   YOUR BOOK IS CALLED WHAT?! | An Introduction
- 10   SHOWER HEADLINES | Drawing Jacob Zuma
- 17   SHAIK, RATTLE & ROLL | November 1997–June 2005
- 36   FATHER OF THE ENTIRE NATION | June 2005–July 2006
- 54   PIRATES OF POLOKWANE | August 2006–September 2008
- 69   GO FOR IT, BOSS | September 2008–April 2009
- 83   DON'T MESS WITH THE PRESIDENT'S HEAD | May 2009–October 2010
- 105   THE LAST SUSHI | October 2010–October 2012
- 132   NUMBER ONE | October 2012–October 2013
- 147   THE CHICKEN RUN | October 2013–March 2015
- 170   RESERVOIR DOGS | May 2015–February 2016
- 186   DEAD PRESIDENT WALKING | March 2016–February 2017
- 209   THE SAXONWOLD SHEBEEN | February 2017–December 2017
- 240   END OF AN ERROR | January 2018 and the aftermath

YOUR BOOK IS CALLED WHAT?!
AN INTRODUCTION

I got a real fright the first time the Sheriff of the Court appeared at the front gate of my Cape Town home in July 2006. "Are you Jonathan Shapiro?" he asked and dropped legal papers on me from Jacob Zuma. My stomach fell through the floor. Zuma was threatening me, and the newspapers that published my cartoons, with R15m in damages and a truckload of legal costs. He and his lawyers weren't known for playing nice. I was deeply anxious about the impact on my family and my future. The trigger for that first lawsuit was a set of cartoons about Zuma's rape trial which he claimed had damaged his reputation.

  I think this was some kind of world record for a cartoonist being sued. R15m for three cartoons – R5m per cartoon! That total was around $2m at the time and the highest I could trace anywhere else was $1m. It felt bizarre, worrying and a bit flattering all at the same time. Thankfully my editors, my lawyers and my family stood firm and soon it became a way of life that Zuma was targeting me.

  Zuma sued me again in 2008 – in the wake of the hugely controversial Rape of Lady Justice cartoon – the same sheriff served me with a R7m summons. So, when the doorbell rang again in 2010, and I saw the sheriff at the gate, I was less fazed. "Is that arsehole suing me again?" I shouted across the garden and the poor guy cracked up laughing.

  His third visit was to serve an amended summons for the second suit, now inexplicably reduced to a mere R5m.

  In the end, the millions of rands in threats came to nothing because, after six years of bluster, Zuma could not face his day in court and all that would reveal. He backed out at the very last minute in October 2012. Obviously his tactic had been to stretch our legal bills as long and as far as possible while the state outrageously covered his costs. I was really sorry the court action did not proceed – unlike Zuma, I genuinely did want my day in court – because we had assembled what I believe would have been a riveting (and highly amusing) case. His appearance on the witness stand would have been quite a spectacle.

The lawsuits may have come to nothing in the end but they definitely did amount to something. It was an attempt by Zuma to intimidate me and to make me back off. And that was just one part of a far broader agenda to silence the independent media as a whole, and other critics of the president and the party.

Twice I was able to directly confront Zuma about his legal actions against me. He appeared at the Cape Town Press Club in 2006 immediately after he sued me the first time and claimed in his speech to be a champion of the free press. At the end I stood up and asked him, "Why are you suing me if you say you are a champion of the free press?" His reply was so vacuous and evasive that I cannot remember exactly what he said. He bluffed his way around it.

The other encounter was on radio in 2008 after he sued me the second time over the Rape of Lady Justice cartoon. When Zuma was on Redi Tlhabi's show on 702 and Cape Talk, I phoned in and asked the same question. His reply this time was memorable: "I saw your cartoons and they are invading my dignity." I wrote that down and put it on the back of my next book cover. It's a jarringly funny metaphor, but also deliciously ironic from a man so palpably lacking in dignity in almost everything he did.

There were plenty of other moments during the Zuma rollercoaster ride when my cartoons became part of the story rather just a reflection of it. Some of them were scary like a pro-Zuma crowd in KZN chanting "Who is the rapist now? Zapiro's the rapist now". And one of those moments seemed almost surreal in its seriousness, although I was completely unaware of it at the time. It came in late 2007 when acting National Prosecuting Authority (NPA) head Mokotedi Mpshe fatefully decided not to charge Zuma during the run-up to the Polokwane ANC elective conference. Mpshe feared that to move against Zuma at that time would destabilise the Scorpions, the NPA and the country. Mpshe much later told Advocate Billy Downer, who prosecuted the Shaik case, that one of his reasons for the decision to delay was a cartoon of mine showing Mpshe pursuing Zuma. He was so worried about being perceived as personally hounding Zuma that he held off.

I have no idea of the true extent of the influence of the cartoon but it represents one of the weirdest intersections between reality and my parallel cartooning universe that I have ever experienced.

The role of cartoonists in our democracy wasn't always this confrontational.

Nelson Mandela seemed to relish being cartooned, warts and all. He viewed an exhibition of my work at his Foundation and I presented him with signed cartoons at his Transkei home in 2004.

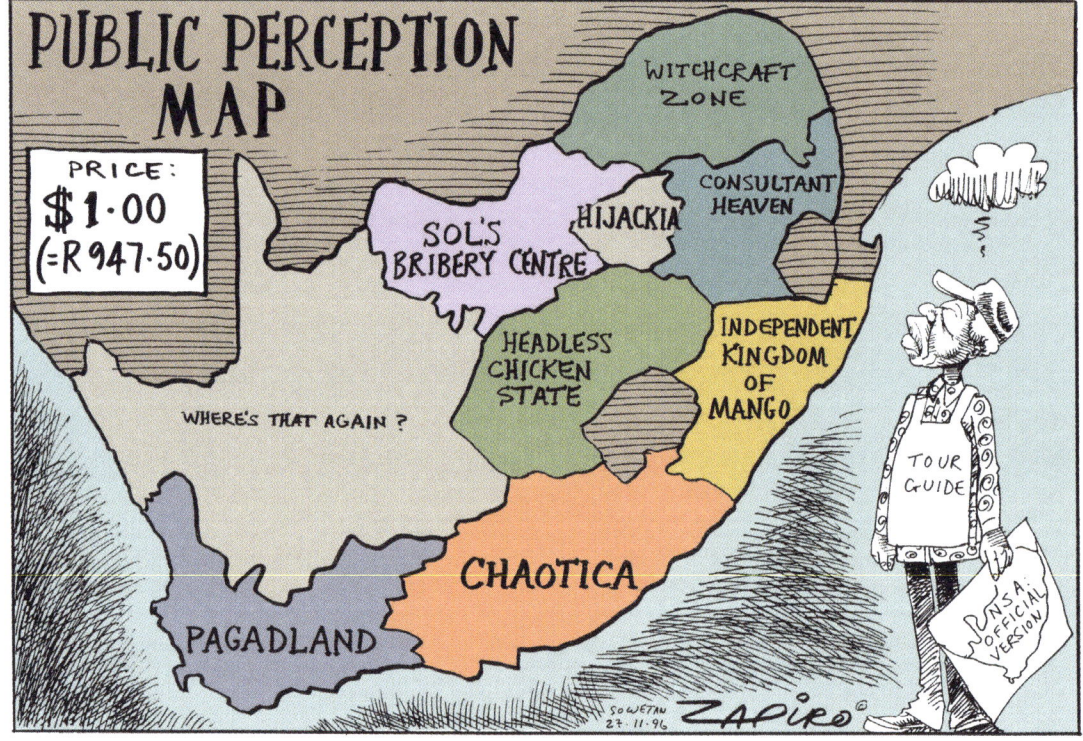

I had several personal encounters with him where he told me he enjoyed my work. He even rang me in 1997. At first I thought it was a prank call. "I am very upset with you," he said. Now I was worried. "I'm upset because I won't be seeing your cartoons every day anymore when I am in Cape Town." He had seen the announcement in the *Cape Argus* that the paper would no longer be running my cartoons. We chatted briefly and I explained that, in the three years since 1994, I'd found myself having to take a more critical stance towards the ANC, him and the government. "Oh, but that is your job," he replied. I've never had a more meaningful endorsement of my role as a cartoonist.

Thabo Mbeki was a very different president. Austere and calculating, he never seemed to show a sense of humour. My personal exchanges with him were polite but distant. I acknowledge that I was brutal in my cartooning of Mbeki at times — especially over the AIDS issue, which I was furious about — but, to his credit, he never threatened me or any other cartoonist.

I had thought and hoped that Nelson Mandela would be the defining figure of my cartooning career but it reflects the dispiriting journey of the nation that Zuma and his showerhead are what come immediately to mind for most when they think of my work. It is telling that ten out of the 22 books (annuals and collections) I have produced have Zuma on the cover while just six have Madiba.

This book tracks my experience, and my cartooning, of the hectic, crazy, weird and sinister rollercoaster ride on which Zuma, and his pals the Guptas, took me, and all of us.

Originally I was going to call this book 'The Poephol Shall Govern' — referencing a 2015 cartoon which you can find on page 171 — but in the end I went with *WTF*.

It says a lot about Jacob Zuma that the choice for a book title about his rise and fall should be between a poephol and WTF.

AN INTRODUCTION | 9

SHOWER HEADLINES
DRAWING JACOB ZUMA

All good political cartooning is somewhat blunt, often harsh and very opinionated. It can be hurtful and for that reason I have to stand and cop whatever criticism comes my way. I don't hide away from that. But I believe cartooning remains one of the most powerful, accessible and creative ways of reporting, communicating, interpreting and campaigning. It has a huge role to play in our political landscape.

Cartoons deal in the hypothetical, the 'what ifs?', and in hyperbole, where things are taken (and drawn) to extremes.

Events in this cartoon world are often either triumphant or despairing. That's what I mean about the hypothetical, especially in the case of Jacob Zuma who swung between those extremes more than anyone else I have ever cartooned. One day the inevitable hypothetical was that he was doomed – he should be in the dustbin of political history and that's what I drew because that's what should have happened and I took the readers on that journey. Then the next day, he survived and even thrived – he had not received his comeuppance and that's what I cartooned. It didn't make the first cartoon wrong – it was just a reflection of the constantly wild oscillations of Zuma's life.

When I draw someone, I am looking for a combination of their distinctive personal features (to draw to an emphatic extreme) and my attitude towards them. As their behaviour, and my attitude towards them, changes, so do the cartoons.

When I first drew Jacob Zuma in 1996, I had never seen him in the flesh and he was not a prominent figure in the media world — or at least the media that reached me. In that pre-internet age, I had to rely on the occasional TV news appearance or a picture in the paper to develop my characterisations.

I didn't know much about Zuma beyond that he was a former trade unionist with little formal education but with political cred as a Robben Islander, a former leader of the ANC's underground operations and a courageous peacemaker in the ANC–IFP KwaZulu-Natal bloodshed.

I portrayed him behind Cyril Ramaphosa in a line of possible challengers to Thabo Mbeki, the heir apparent to the ANC leadership when Mandela stepped down in 1997. I did notice something about the egg-like symmetry of Zuma's head and worked off that. I had no strong view of him and he was a bit player in this cartoon, so his was a less developed figure than Mandela, Mbeki, Ramaphosa and Tokyo Sexwale. He also was younger and more hirsute than we see him now.

Soon the double bump would become the distinctive feature of my cartoons of him.

The more I draw any person, the more I build the characterisation out. I study the image closely and re-work it. As Zuma's behaviour got worse, my cartooning hardened and his squinting eyeballs and tooth gap became shifty features to work with.

One day I was examining Zuma's face and I thought, "Wait, there are actually two heads in there!" ... which worked well when he appointed Moe Shaik as his intelligence head.

No doubt it was the head bump that was the dominant feature of my cartooning of him until his trial for rape in 2006, when he gave that preposterous testimony that he had taken a shower after sex with Khwezi, whom he knew to be HIV positive, in order to reduce his chances of getting AIDS.

I first drew a shower in connection with Zuma, but not connected to his head, in one panel of an eight-panel cartoon during that trial in April 2006. I had no thought in my mind that this was the start of something iconic.

Two days later the shower was attached to his head for the first time.

For two months the showerhead came and went but readers kept asking for it to be restored. And I realised I had stumbled onto something. I have long been a fan of the great English cartoonist Steve Bell, who famously drew Prime Minister John Major all the time with his underpants outside his trousers. It became a signature piece of his work.

I thought the showerhead for Zuma could be my equivalent and from September 2006 it became a fixture.

There was a brief reprieve at the start of the Zuma presidency in 2009 when we had, what depressingly proved to be, a false dawn of good governance. I felt Zuma deserved a sort of clean slate so I put the showerhead in hover mode above him, to wait and see what would emerge. I genuinely hoped I would be able to take it away.

DRAWING JACOB ZUMA | 13

The reprieve lasted less than a year. Come SONA in February 2010, the showerhead was back forever.

Over the past 12 years I have drawn the showerhead as a nose, a rhino horn, a pennywhistle, a zipline hook, the letter 'f', a snorkel, a spy camera, a fitting on top of the Eiffel Tower, a spray, a soap dispenser, a vacuum cleaner, a vuvuzela, a gate decoration, a piece of armour, a weapon, a lamplight, a telephone, a speaker, a drain ... and a penis.

I even gave Donald Trump a golden version.

The showerhead took on a life of its own and became a symbol at protests.
  Someone took a showerhead to the Gupta mansion in Saxonwold. And it began appearing in all kinds of strange places.

I was also told, on what I would describe as good authority, that South African sign language interpreters for the deaf were using a gesture of the showerhead to mean Zuma. When I repeated that story in public, some official body immediately denied it, claiming the gesture reflected Zuma's prominent forehead. Yeh, right. Several years later I was told that young kids at a school for the hearing-impaired were all using the showerhead gesture to indicate the president.

Even Julius Malema adopted it as a visual gesture of constant mockery.

I created a Zuma figurine with the showerhead in place. And one of Malema responding.

Somehow Zuma could never shake that showerhead and all that it came to represent — sexism, ignorance, corruption, abuse of power and incompetence.

SHAIK, RATTLE & ROLL
NOVEMBER 1997–JUNE 2005

At the 1997 ANC elective conference in Mafikeng, Thabo Mbeki comfortably saw off all other contenders for the leadership crown, cleverly outmanoeuvring Cyril Ramaphosa who was Mandela's favoured candidate. Jacob Zuma became deputy president of the party after a late attempt to nominate Winnie Madikizela-Mandela against him failed on procedural grounds. In 1999 he became deputy president of the country. He was appointed head of the nation's Moral Regeneration Movement (how ironic that title would become!) and he was very much in the shadow of the formidable Mbeki.

Zuma then was an underestimated figure, a mistake many would repeat over the next two decades. He did, however, play a role as a mediator in justifying Robert Mugabe's theft of the 2002 Zimbabwean election from Morgan Tsvangirai's MDC — all part of Mbeki's 'quiet diplomacy' policy.

 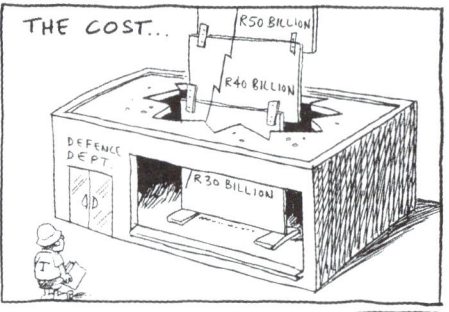

The Arms Deal had been a running sore for the ANC government since the massive weapons procurement programme was first conceived during Nelson Mandela's government. It was plain to see that involvement in this kind of business would inevitably be a corrupting influence. The idea that arms sales could be conducted with 'reputable customers only', and that the amorality that usually accompanies these kinds of transactions could be avoided, demonstrated an unfortunate naivety on Mandela's part.

As the arms trade snowballed, ethics were trampled in the scramble for kickbacks. Defence minister Joe Modise, in particular, became involved in some appallingly corrupt deals. The ANC was on the defensive.

The chief of acquisitions for the defence force was Shamim 'Chippy' Shaik. In October 2001, Chippy was suspended (and later axed) for leaking Arms Deal info to his brother Schabir, who was bidding for some of the action. Schabir had been a generous backer and financial advisor of Zuma when he returned from exile and during his time as MEC for Economic Affairs and Tourism in KZN.

Chippy and Schabir were only two of four brothers who had great influence in the ANC from their struggle days, and who would all attract controversy. Chippy was also found to have falsified some of his qualifications. Schabir would, briefly, go to jail for corruption. Moe would play a big role in trying to smear prosecutions boss Bulelani Ngcuka. And Yunus was accused of fabricating defences of his brothers and exerting undue political influence on behalf of Jacob Zuma as a board member of eTV's holding company. All the brothers would appear unflatteringly in many of my cartoons in the next decade although Yunus was very amiable when I met him at a bar mitzvah, of all places. I also once had a friendly phone call from him about how pleased he had been to receive a signed copy of this cartoon. Was that narcissism or a healthy sense of humour? I am not sure.

The elite Scorpions investigations unit began to probe whether Zuma had solicited a R500,000 bribe from Thales, a French company linked to the Arms Deal, through Schabir Shaik.

By the 2002 ANC conference, Zuma was already considered damaged goods. I was portraying him as corrupt five years before he would take over the ANC leadership and 16 long years before he would finally fall from power. Naively, I and many others thought, at the time, that he was already fatally compromised.

But Zuma developed his trademark response of ducking, diving, delaying and smearing his way out of trouble, helped by official incompetence or reluctance. Little did I know that we were settling in for 15 years of this shit. And little did I know that the buffalo, which Zuma is portrayed as here, would later come to symbolise his rival and successor, Cyril Ramaphosa.

As transport minister, Mac Maharaj had also received shady payments from Shaik.

The Arms Deal claimed its first major victim when struggle luminary Tony Yengeni copped a five-year sentence for fraudulently concealing from parliament a massive discount on a 4x4 vehicle he received from a company linked to the Arms Deal.

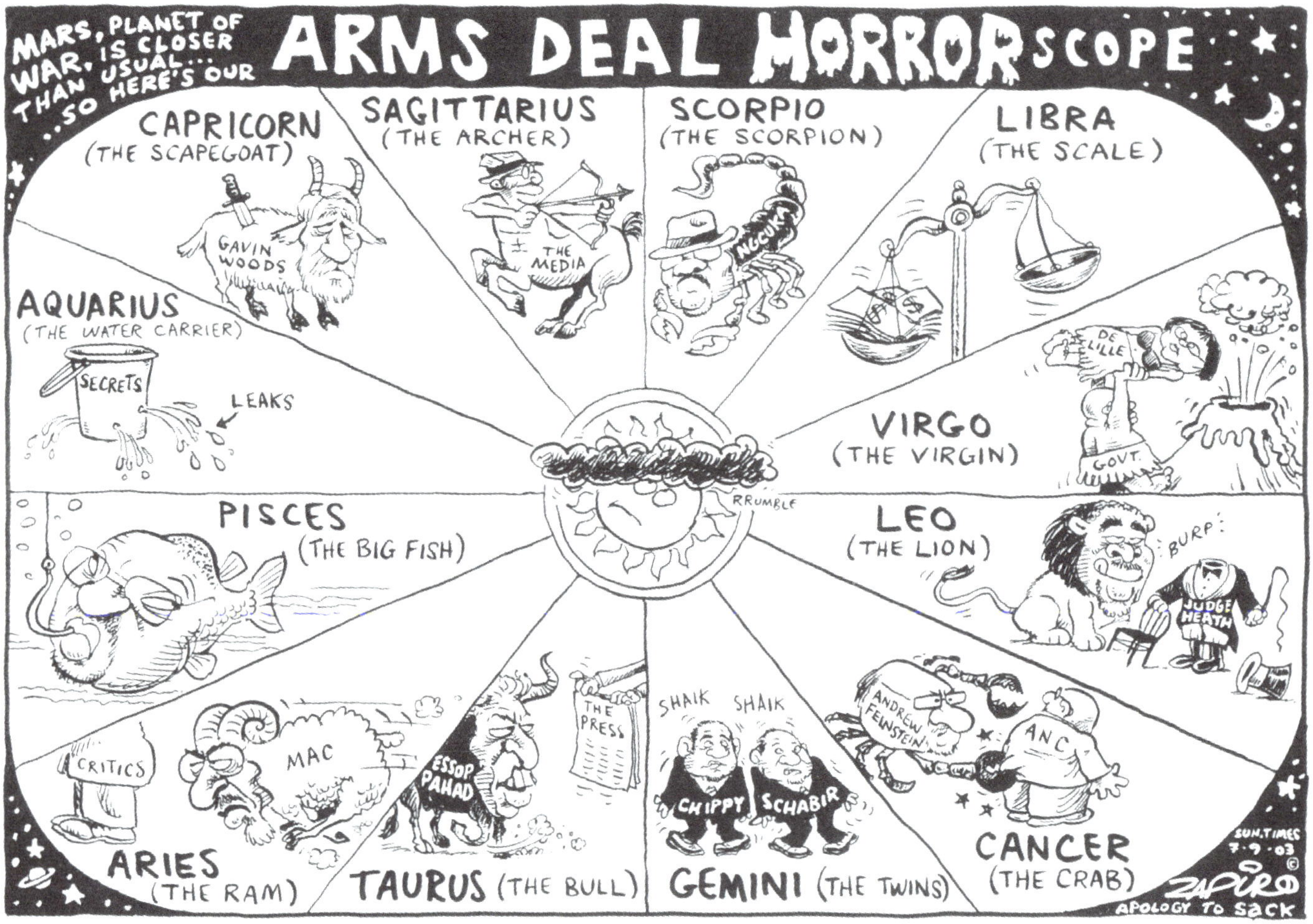

By September 2003, Zuma and the allegations against him, which now included undeclared expenses, were dominating the national psyche.

Early in 2004, as strong evidence of Zuma's apparent corruption mounted, I sent *Mail & Guardian* editor Mondli Makhanya a rough draft of this cartoon, which was as tough and hard-hitting as any I would ever do. He immediately phoned me and, without even saying hello, said, "You are one sick motherf%#*er" (which might become the title of my autobiography). He told me he couldn't run the cartoon but asked me not to use it anywhere else. "So, you mean it might get bad enough to run it?" I asked. He replied "maybe".

Six months later my phone rang and, once again without even saying hello, Mondli's distinctive voice simply said, "It's time."

The trigger for publishing the cartoon was National Prosecuting Authority head Bulelani Ngcuka's fateful, clumsy announcement in August 2004: "We have concluded that, whilst there is a prima facie case of corruption against the deputy president, our prospects of success are not strong enough. That means that we are not sure if we have a winnable case. Accordingly, we have decided not to prosecute the deputy president."

Zuma was outraged at the 'prima facie case' statement. In a classic intelligence operative manoeuvre, an anonymous e-mail smeared Ngcuka. Maharaj and Moe Shaik claimed he was an apartheid spy and the Hefer Commission was set up by Thabo Mbeki to investigate.

Explaining his struggle history to the commission, Ngcuka made reference to the fact that he had been in detention with me in 1988 (we were only together briefly before being split up on racial grounds). "Maybe that's why he draws me so much," he said.

Hefer found the spy claims to be completely baseless and that the accusers had even hooked up with notorious former apartheid agents in trying to nail Ngcuka.

But the pressure got to Ngcuka and he resigned.

Schabir Shaik went on trial in the Durban High Court in October 2004 for Arms Deal charges of fraud and his alleged corruption of Zuma. Bizarrely, Zuma was not in court beside him.

NOVEMBER 1997–JUNE 2005 | 29

A central document in the case was an encrypted fax sent to Paris which allegedly set out a bribe agreement between Shaik, Zuma and Alain Thetard of Thales.

After intense legal debate, the controversial fax was admitted in evidence.

In spite of his legal problems, it still seemed distinctly possible that Zuma would become our head of state one day. It was *Sunday Times* editor Ray Hartley who sparked this prescient and ominous long-range peek into our depressing future.

Judge Hilary Squires took three days to deliver his judgment – all of it broadcast live to the nation.

THE VERDICT: JOIN THE DOTS

Shaik was found guilty on all counts and sentenced to an effective 15 years for corruption and fraud. He would only serve two years before receiving medical parole for a terminal illness which he has miraculously survived in a remarkably healthy state to this day.

Judge Squires was widely reported as finding that a 'generally corrupt relationship' existed between Zuma and Shaik. (He would, much later, correct the record and the words 'mutually beneficial symbiosis' would be used instead.) The implications for Zuma seemed catastrophic. When the 'dots' cartoon was published, several senior ANC MPs were seen in parliament surreptitiously joining the dots in barely concealed copies of the *Mail & Guardian*.

The Tripartite Alliance youth movements and the populist left had been alienated by Mbeki, so they delivered vociferous support for Zuma.

Zuma resigned as an MP but declined to resign as deputy president. Characteristically, Mbeki moved slowly on the issue. He even headed off overseas for a while. At the World Economic Forum in Cape Town during this period, the president spoke some fine words about fighting corruption. I introduced myself at the plenary and asked him, "You have been talking about corruption, what are you going to do about your deputy president?" He gave me a withering look (Mbeki was very good at withering looks), and said, "I am sure Zapiro knows what I am going to say. It's a long judgment which needs to be scrutinised properly ... etc, etc" and he finished with another withering look and said, "And I am sure Zapiro knew I was going to say that."

After 12 days of intense speculation, Mbeki called a special sitting of parliament to announce that he had sacked Zuma and replaced him with Phumzile Mlambo-Ngcuka, the wife of the former NPA boss who had declared there was a prima facie case against Zuma.

FATHER OF THE ENTIRE NATION

JUNE 2005–JULY 2006

Zuma remained deputy president of the ANC and, without any official government duties, was free to launch a textbook populist fightback portraying himself as the victim of a political conspiracy.

He told anyone who would listen that he only wanted his day in court. Until the new NPA boss, Vusi Pikoli, announced that he would indeed be charged.

I respected Cosatu leader Zwelinzima Vavi but his decision to double down on his support for Zuma, to propagate conspiracy theories and to abet the undermining of the justice system in order to regain influence on government, was palpably wrong. It was a decision he would later deeply regret and recant.

Zuma finally did appear on corruption charges. His lawyers delayed proceedings at every chance while in public Zuma questioned the legitimacy of the court. He sang what became his signature song *'Awuleth' Umshini Wami'* ('bring me my machine gun') and his unruly supporters burned T-shirts with Mbeki's image.

Zuma was now in open conflict with Mbeki, quoting Chairman Mao in a barely veiled reference to a 'paper leader' rather than the people's choice.

Ahead of his third court appearance, his shady backers held a fundraising party.

Then Zuma faced a startling new allegation from an entirely different direction. He was charged with the rape of a 31-year-old daughter of a family friend, later known as Khwezi, who had been a guest at his home.

Cosatu leadership said the new charge might make them re-consider their support for Zuma.

Many of his previous supporters were now having serious doubts. Among those I drew jumping out of the Zuma plane in this cartoon was the respected senior SACP figure and later cabinet minister Jeremy Cronin. This cartoon upset Cronin who, when he saw me later, insisted that he had "never been on that plane in the first place". He said he had not been a supporter of Zuma. It was an exchange which made me think how strange it was that my cartoon universe was sometimes being analysed in great detail in high places and sometimes taken almost literally.

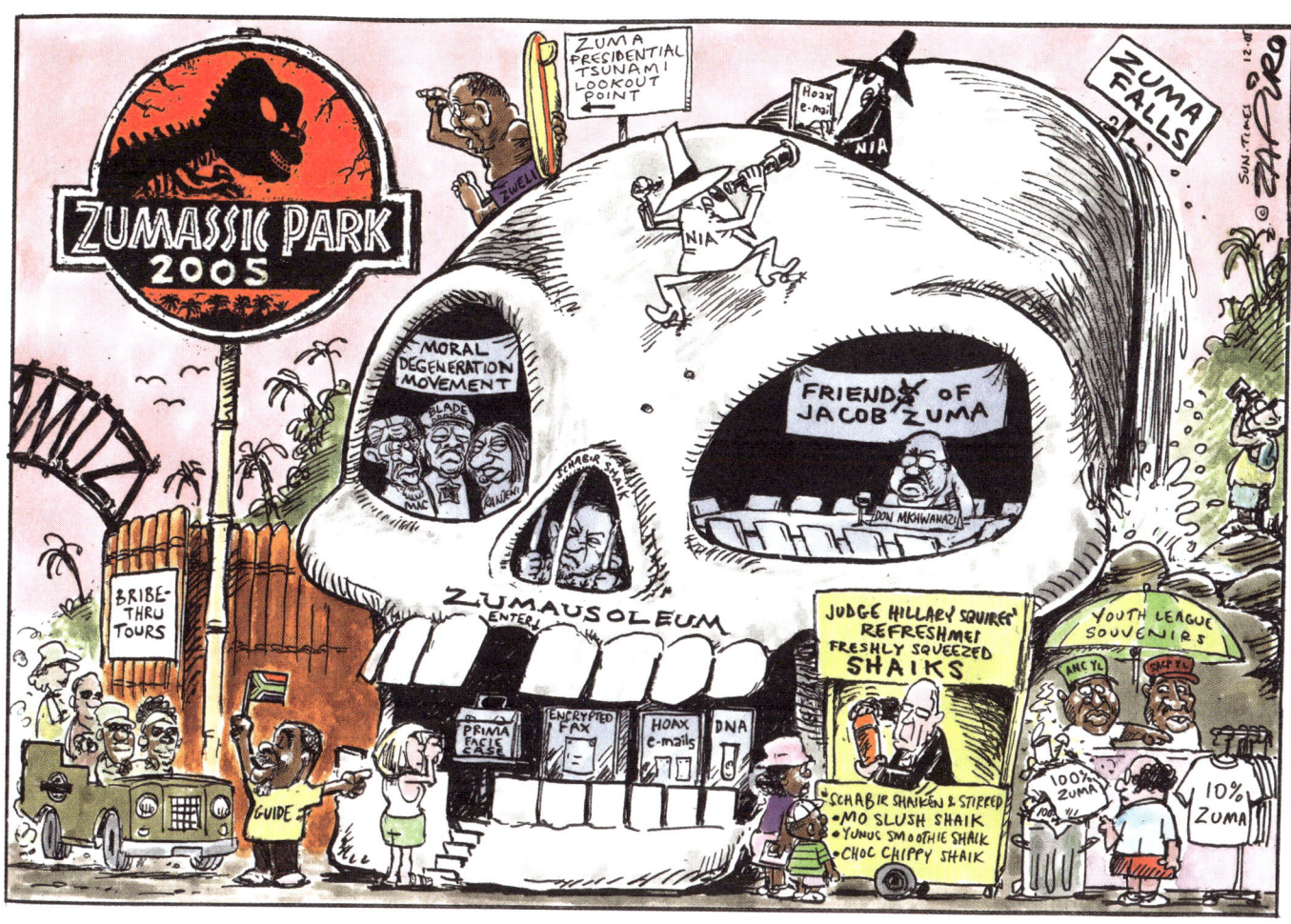

Thabo Mbeki now couldn't escape Zuma's presence whether he was officially opening the new Southern African Large Telescope (SALT) in the Karoo or launching the party's local government election manifesto.

Zuma had three wives, an ex-wife and many offspring (so many that no reporter had an exact number). He admitted he had unprotected sex with his rape accuser. Then a judge recused himself from the rape trial because Zuma had fathered that judge's nephew.

Outside court, Zuma's supporters behaved abysmally – burning pictures of Khwezi and shouting "Burn the bitch". Zuma stirred it all up with his signature song.

Inside the courtroom, there was a sense that, because she had had the temerity to pursue this case, Khwezi was the one who was on trial. She got a rough ride from Zuma's lawyer Kemp J Kemp. (That name always tickled me and later I imagined Kemp Kemp appearing in front of Mogoeng Mogoeng.)

And then Zuma took the stand himself. This was the first of three cartoons that were later cited in Zuma's initial lawsuit against me. In their court papers, his lawyers said that this cartoon implied that their client would either lie on the witness stand or was a habitual liar. I had no problem with that statement!

Zuma's evidence included astonishing statements from a man allegedly responsible for the government's AIDS prevention programme and also the official head of the Moral Regeneration Movement. He testified that he interpreted Khwezi wearing a kanga as an invitation for sex. He had unprotected sex with her even though he knew her to be HIV positive. He said he had taken a shower afterwards in order to reduce his chances of getting AIDS.

This was the second cartoon cited in the lawsuit and again the lawyers' papers amused me as they went into great detail about the indignity faced by their client being drawn naked with his trousers around his ankles.

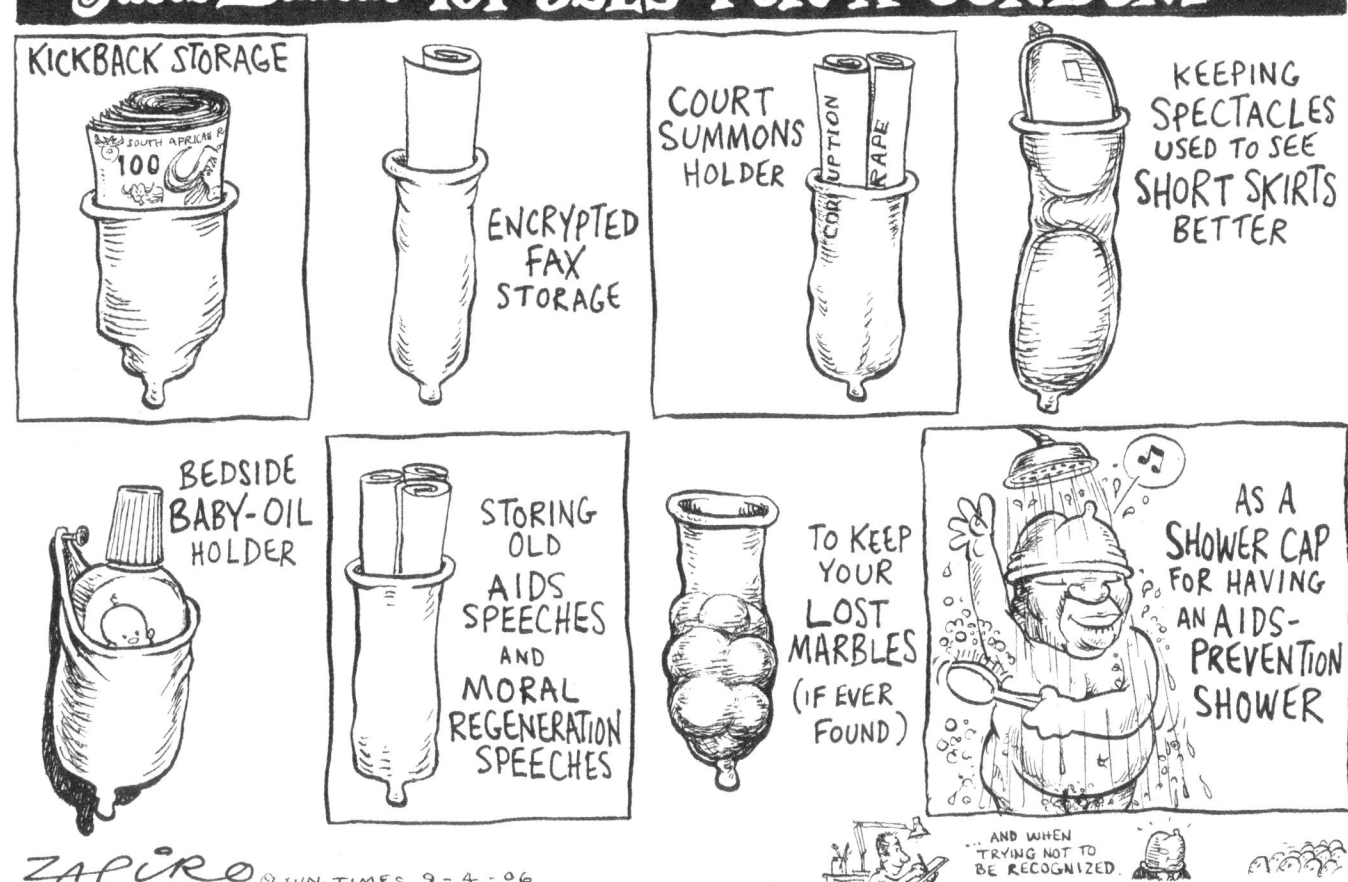

The image of a shower in connection with Jacob Zuma appeared for the first time in one small panel. I had no idea then how that would grow into something powerfully symbolic. Within two months it was to become a permanent fixture on his head.

There was plenty of intelligence services' mischief going on in support of Zuma with the bugging of politicians' phones and a hoax e-mail campaign – seemingly the work of director-general Billy Masetlha ... who was then sacked.

Zuma, and the nation, awaited the televised trial verdict with genuine uncertainty. This cartoon provoked a very strong reaction.

Zuma was acquitted but chastised by the judge for being unable to control his sexual urges. He celebrated outside court with his supporters. My reflection of that moment was the third cartoon cited in the lawsuit.

At a subsequent media conference Zuma denied that he had ever said that a shower could prevent HIV.

The ANC Youth League propagated a wild conspiracy theory that the rape accused (dubbed Lucifer) was bribed to lay the charge, helped by the 'evil hands' of Bulelani Ngcuka and intelligence minister Ronnie Kasrils.

Graphically, this remains my favourite cover of all the 22 annuals I have produced.

At the National Union of Mineworkers' conference, its president, Senzeni Zokwana, said Christians shouldn't judge Zuma and that the Ten Commandments meant nothing to his union.

NUM's edited TEN COMMANDMENTS

Thou shalt have no other gods before Jacob Zuma.

Thou shalt not take the name of Zuma in vain, even when he talks bull about showers.

Thou shalt not make any graven image or earthly likeness, especially those goggle-eyed bump-headed J.Z. cartoons.

Thou shalt not kill His chance for a shot at the Top Job.

Thou shalt not commit adultery with a potential honey-trap.

Thou shalt not steal, except for legitimate strike looting.

Thou shalt not bear false witness against thy neighbour, unless thy neighbour is Kasrils or Ngcuka.

Thou shalt not covet thy neighbour's house, nor his ass, but his wife's ass is fair game.

In July 2006 Zuma lawsuits started flying against seven people or media entities. The total amount was for R62m. My share was the biggest at R15m. Not a cent of that R62m was ever won by Zuma – he much later abandoned all the suits.

This cartoon was my first response to the lawsuit. I remember my editors trying to dissuade me, in consultation with lawyers, from re-publishing (in miniature) the three cartoons that I was being sued for. But I was determined and went ahead.

PIRATES OF POLOKWANE
AUGUST 2006–SEPTEMBER 2008

Somehow, in spite of everything, Zuma had in political terms survived the shameful rape trial and the fraud and corruption charges. The latter had been thrown out for the moment on procedural grounds and, although there was a possibility they could be reinstated, the only serious threat to his chances of succeeding Thabo Mbeki seemed to lie in the rumoured candidacy of Cyril Ramaphosa.

Ultimately, Ramaphosa stayed out of the race and we were starting to come to terms with the bewildering likelihood of a Zuma presidency in 2009.

Zuma spoke out against gay marriage saying same-sex unions "should not be tolerated in any normal society".

I, and others being sued by Zuma, recognised an own goal when we saw one – Zuma wanted damages because his reputation had been damaged but, in his desperation to paint a rosy picture, he publicly declared that his image was intact!

The isolated Thabo Mbeki totally failed to read the mood and was determined to stand again as president of the party in 2007 even though the constitution would not allow him to remain president of the nation after 2009. Large sections of the party, especially in Zuma strongholds like KZN, were openly hostile to him.

Nelson Mandela, as the elder statesman, tried and failed to bridge the deepening party divide.

Zuma displayed an uncanny ability to say whatever appealed to whoever was listening at the time without ever reconciling the obvious contradictions and conflicts in his statements.

The succession debate became all-consuming and Cosatu confirmed its preferred choice for the December voting in Polokwane.

Mbeki may have been out of touch, arrogant and responsible for calamitous AIDS policies, but he was never accused of personal corruption. There were plenty of allegations about money from the Arms Deal that he may (or may not) have orchestrated for the ANC's funds but not for himself. His reputation as a conscientious technocrat remained intact ... which made his loyalty to his patently corrupt police chief Jackie Selebi all the stranger. Mbeki strenuously, and at great cost to the justice system, tried to protect Selebi from serious charges which ultimately did send him to jail.

With the choice seemingly between rampant populism and increasing authoritarianism, many still held out some futile hope that Ramaphosa, late in the day, would enter the fray.

Mbeki and his close allies were in a bubble — they seemed like the only people in the ANC who did not understand how far Zuma was ahead in any likely ballot. He had five of the nine provinces officially backing him. Only the filing of new corruption and fraud charges seemingly could trip him up. Acting NPA head Mokotedi Mpshe was known to be considering his options. He decided that charging Zuma so close to the Polokwane conference would seem like a political act, so he held off. As described in the introduction to this book, I was astonished to learn eight years later that this cartoon may have played a role in that decision by Mpshe. He was embarrassed about being portrayed as hounding Zuma.

Two weeks before the big vote, I was pretty certain which way we were heading.

Mbeki took a brutal pasting at Polokwane. Zuma's slate swept the board and his supporters rowdily dominated the floor against the national backdrop of regular Eskom outages.

Now that his succession was guaranteed, Zuma's constantly confusing policy utterances immediately came under closer scrutiny. Some, like Zwelinzima Vavi, were quickly disillusioned.

Zuma was not yet on the throne but he was controlling power behind the scenes and his first priority was to destroy or emasculate the organs of state which had prosecuted him. And to undermine the judicial system. The elite Scorpions, an FBI-style unit founded by Mbeki in 1999 to fight high-profile corruption cases, were disbanded by safety and security minister Charles Nqakula, who was eager to please his new boss ... and Jackie Selebi, who had also been investigated by them.

Revenge was in the air. Mbeki supporters were about to be aggressively rooted out of positions in the party, the government and state-owned enterprises.

It was an ominous time. The looting that became State Capture, and the ANC's facilitation of it in the name of blind loyalty to their leader, still hadn't happened. But, to me, it now seemed inevitable. Looking back, it is scary how these two cartoons, which might have seemed hyperbolic at the time, proved to be depressingly prophetic.

AUGUST 2006–SEPTEMBER 2008 | 67

On one major controversial issue, both sides of the party remained hopelessly compromised.

As we dreaded the impending accession to power of a deeply flawed old man, in the United States a youthful and principled orator was transforming his nation's politics.

GO FOR IT, BOSS
SEPTEMBER 2008–APRIL 2009

What became known as the Rape of Lady Justice cartoon appeared in the *Sunday Times* on 7 September 2008 ahead of Judge Nicholson pronouncing on whether the National Prosecuting Authority's corruption case against Jacob Zuma could proceed. Of all the cartoons I have ever done, this one provoked by far the greatest response. It was attacked, praised, debated and analysed on public platforms, on TV, on radio, in newspapers and in huge volumes on blogs and online media. The controversy surrounding the cartoon was covered in many international media, including the BBC, Al Jazeera, the *New York Times* and *LA Times*.

The cartoon was the subject of formal complaints to the Human Rights Commission and would soon draw a legal suit from Zuma. Thanks to those legal proceedings, I have a detailed record of exactly how this cartoon came about in the form of my affidavits and submissions.

Prior to the case, Zuma and his allies had threatened the judiciary alarmingly. Among other things: Julius Malema infamously said he'd kill for Zuma (if the court case went ahead); Zuma was present on the same platform when Malema said this and did nothing to deny this threat when it was his turn to speak; Zwelinzima Vavi had echoed Malema in saying he too would kill for Zuma (and for the same reason); Gwede Mantashe called Constitutional Court judges counter-revolutionaries and said there'd be anarchy if the court case went ahead; SACP general secretary Blade Nzimande stated that if Zuma was required to stand trial it would take the country to the brink.

The initial draft of the cartoon was prepared on 4 September 2008, the day Cosatu announced a two-day national strike if Judge Nicholson ruled against Zuma. I viewed that as a further attempt to bully the court.

The process I usually follow when preparing a cartoon is this: I write down various subjects, then I write down my attitudes towards those subjects, and then I link the subjects and attitudes with arrows and create a mind map before, lastly, considering the best method to visually portray what I have put down in words. In my view, Zuma and his supporters were determinedly and systematically undermining the entire legal system until charges against him were dropped or the courts ruled in his favour. But how to portray that? When brainstorming the idea, I wrote down the words Zuma was 'raping the justice system'. It suddenly occurred to me that the metaphorical figure of justice was a woman and that all the main role players were male. The first rough drawing came to me in one swift concept, unlike the way my ideas usually develop. Part of what I wanted to depict in the cartoon was that Zuma wasn't doing much of the talking himself. His supporters were making most of the damaging statements concerning the judiciary and effectively egging him on. So, even though he was the prime rapist of the system, the others were facilitating the attack in a manner similar to a gang rape. The reason why Mantashe is the one speaking is that he represents the ANC, which I saw as the other prime assailant of the justice system. Zuma's own trial for rape – at which he was found not guilty – was genuinely an afterthought and it was background and not foreground to the cartoon. I immediately knew it was a strong idea. But was it too strong?

I did a clearer rough draft and faxed it to Mondli Makhanya, who was now *Sunday Times* editor. He was at a restaurant. He phoned me back immediately to say, "Yoh! Yoh! Yoh! I told the waiter, who was as black as me, to expect a fax and I saw him pick it up and, as he looked at the cartoon, I swear he turned white."

Mondli, a fearless editor, was prepared to run the cartoon but I was worried, not about what everyone in the drawing might think (although I had some sympathy for Vavi), but because of how women might view it. I tested the cartoon on two female colleagues who were experienced journalists. They were taken aback but felt it was right. So we went with it.

The response was extraordinary. My friend and fellow cartoonist Andy Mason penned an article titled 'A Sharp Intake of Breath', which he said was his, and everybody else's, response to the cartoon when they first saw it.

Debate raged about the cartoon's validity.

Every person portrayed in it (except Lady Justice!) attacked it directly but the most worrying criticism for me came from some who said the cartoon fed a prevalent South African stereotype or trope of the black male as a sexual predator. I don't believe that was the case at all. I'm extremely conscious of the racial power imbalance in this country – of white people setting agendas and defining constructs for identity. I think about this a lot. But this drawing is clearly a metaphor and the concept of 'the rape of an institution' is entrenched in language and included in dictionaries. The cartoon entirely reflects Zuma's own behaviour as a powerful politician whose portrayal is defined by his actions and not by his race. And the cartoon is deliberately not graphic in its portrayal – it suggests an event without explicitly portraying it. I later discovered instances from other cartoonists around the world who had used a similar theme and sometimes in a far more graphic way. One thing I remember clearly is that some rape survivors, and even gang rape survivors, from across the racial spectrum, expressed their support for the cartoon.

Within a couple of days of the cartoon being published, both Zuma and Mantashe came out separately with statements saying that they respected the justice system. Many commentators believed that was in direct response to the cartoon. So I refreshed my original concept, this time for the *Mail & Guardian*. And the reaction felt totally different. Perhaps the pious expressions on the protagonists' faces helped but it was noticeable that fewer criticised the cartoon and some, even though the issue was dire, could not help themselves from laughing.

Judge Nicholson ruled that the procedures followed by the NPA were so faulty that the charges, as they were then constituted, had to be dropped and he stated that claims of "political undercurrents" in the process were "not completely unbelievable". While I was concerned about the sweeping nature of Nicholson's findings, I felt the Mbeki camp's abuse of the process was an extremely important point, so I did another version of the original concept.

Zuma and his allies appeared triumphantly on a platform near the Pietermaritzburg High Court and attacked me in various ways. Senior ANC figure Baleka Mbete deliberately and dangerously misrepresented the cartoon, saying to the angry crowd of thousands, "The woman in the cartoon is white. Is Zapiro saying that Zuma will rape white women?" In the drawing Lady Justice clearly has an African appearance, something I have tested on many audiences and readers. (Since 1996, I had been drawing her as a black woman to represent justice in the new South Africa.) Zuma repeated the racial calumny when I later confronted him on radio. He questioned why Lady Justice was white.

What was incredibly heartening for me was the support I received from my fellow South African cartoonists when the furore was raging and when Zuma later sued me.

'Instead of suing a cartoonist, Zuma should try cleaning his tarnished reputation by giving it a good shower.'

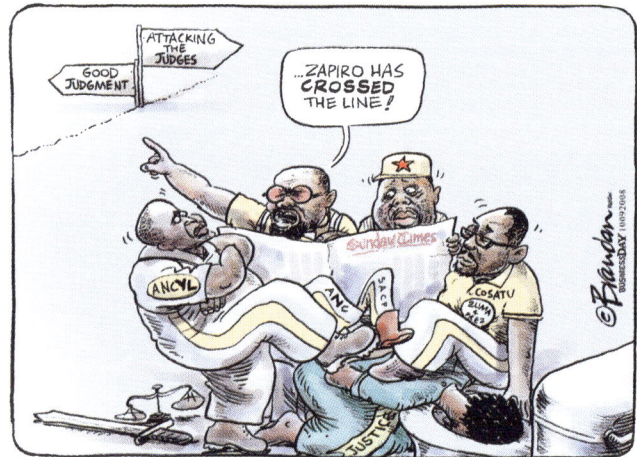

CARTOONISTS FROM LEFT TO RIGHT: Madam & Eve, Chip, Grogan, Brandan and Jeremy Nel.

The Cartoonists Rights Network International rallied the global cartooning community to demonstrate their solidarity, which they did in various wonderful forms from Burkina Faso and Kenya to Colombia, Mexico and beyond.

The CRNI later gave me their annual Award for Courage in Editorial Cartooning at an event in Washington where I found myself sharing a platform with Flemming Rose, the man responsible for publishing the Prophet Muhammad cartoons in the Danish newspaper *Jyllands-Posten* in 2005.

The CRNI reported that they had not come across another democracy where cartoons had played a bigger role in the national discourse than SA during the previous decade.

In May 2013, I was stunned to find the Rape of Justice cartoon had been included in a prestigious collection on BuzzFeed of 'Fifteen Historic Cartoons That Changed the World' compiled by Victor Navasky, former editor of *The Nation* and the author of *The Art of Controversy: Political Cartoons and Their Enduring Power*. My effort squeaked in at number 15! I'm well aware that there's huge hyperbole in that headline. I would never claim that my cartoon changed the world. But it was an incredible feeling to be listed among some of the great cartoons of the past 200 years including work from heroes of mine like Daumier, David Low, David Levine and Art Spiegelman (who mentored me when I studied in New York in 1989).

The Human Rights Commission would rule in June 2010 that the cartoon was "political expression published in the public interest and deserved heightened protection". They said the cartoon was not incitement or hate speech and did not infringe the right to dignity of women or rape victims. The finding did have an odd rider, however. Having exonerated me in their ruling, the commissioners added that they found the cartoon and the words to be "probably distasteful and offensive", which was a curiously subjective expression from an official body.

I remain convinced that the cartoon was entirely justifiable.

CARTOONISTS, TOP TO BOTTOM: Glez (Burkina Faso), Luis (Colombia), Brito (France), Ché (Spain) and Gado (Kenya).

The Nicholson ruling handed Zuma's supporters the excuse they were seeking to remove Thabo Mbeki from power. The judgment would later be brusquely overturned on appeal but, by then, the political damage had long been done.

The ever-inscrutable Mbeki was immediately recalled as president by the ANC and replaced by Kgalema Motlanthe.

Motlanthe's elevation into what was deliberately cast as a caretaker role led to an awkward power balance between him, Zuma and the assertively noisy Julius Malema.

The recall sparked the first significant split in the party of liberation with Mosiuoa Lekota and Mbhazima Shilowa leading the breakaway that became COPE in the face of bitter criticism from Jeff Radebe and other Zuma supporters.

Prosecutions head Vusi Pikoli had been suspended by Mbeki pending a commission of inquiry, which cleared him. President Motlanthe axed him anyway and also resisted calls for an Arms Deal inquiry.

Nicholson's judgment, used as the excuse to recall Mbeki, was overturned by the Supreme Court of Appeal and the charges against Zuma were reinstated. Nicholson had overstepped — he had included things in his judgment that were outside the ambit of the case. However, as already noted, the political consequences of his ruling did not have any appeal process.

SEPTEMBER 2008–APRIL 2009 | 79

SONA in 2009 was an awkward event for a presidential bench-warmer while everyone was anticipating the election that lay two months ahead.

ANC spokesman Carl Niehaus was revealed to have a trail of bad debt, forged signatures and broken promises. He resigned yet would somehow remain a persistent fly in our political ointment for many years to come.

In a massive call, acting NPA head Mokotedi Mpshe in April 2009 dropped the charges against Zuma citing "intolerable abuse" of the process. The decision was based on what became known as the spy tapes — recordings anonymously supplied to Zuma's legal team in which former Scorpions head Leonard McCarthy is heard trying to manipulate the timing of the charges.

Assisting Mpshe in this process was his deputy, Willie Hofmeyr, who was an old mentor, table tennis partner and friend of mine. When I was in detention he was in the cell next to me. This cartoon, and the one that follows it, were painful for him. He phoned me months later and said in effect: "I wish you could know what I know. I wish you could know why." It was a difficult conversation but I said I couldn't cartoon on the basis of things that were hidden. This was how the story looked to me.

SEPTEMBER 2008–APRIL 2009 | 81

In April 2009 our fourth democratic election produced an outcome that was both inevitable and unbelievable.

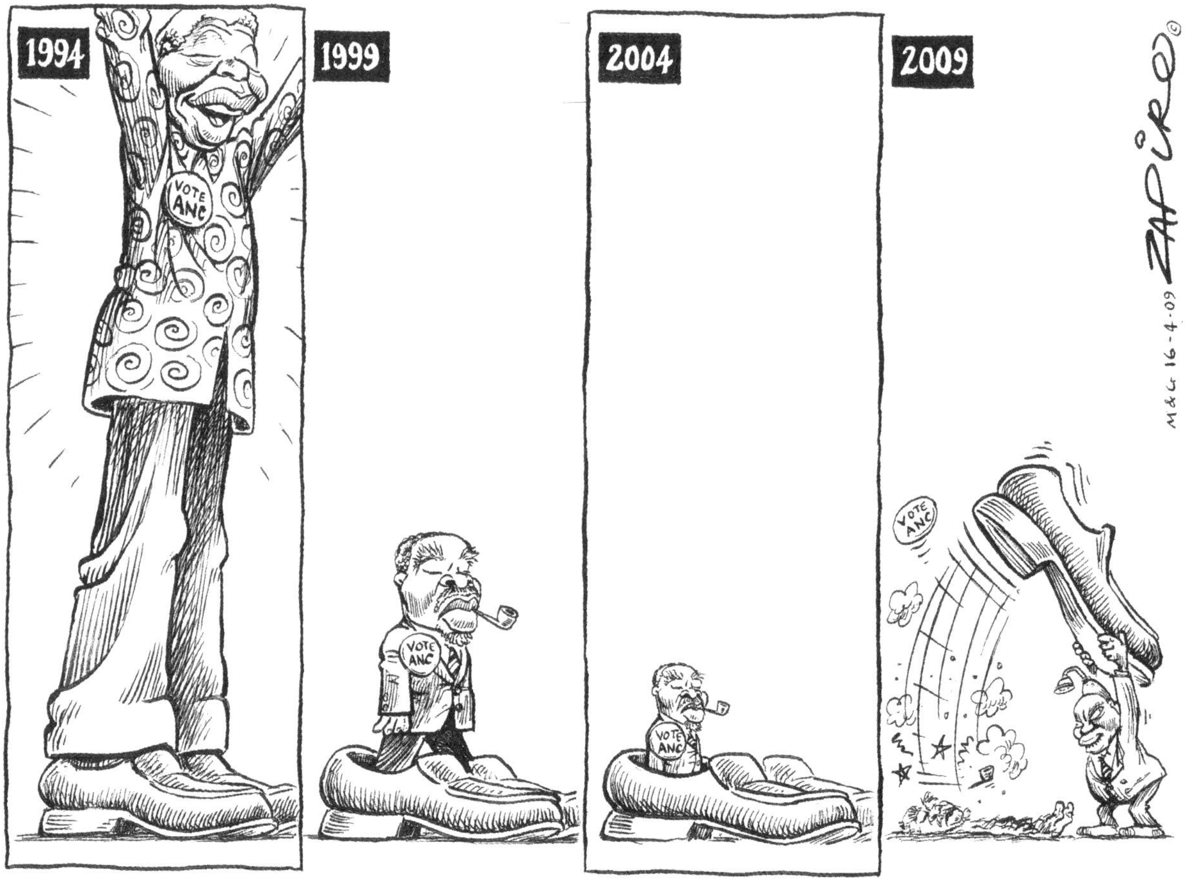

DON'T MESS WITH THE PRESIDENT'S HEAD

MAY 2009–OCTOBER 2010

Somehow this deeply compromised man had won the political game and was to officially become South Africa's president. I had already drawn the Watershed Moment cartoon ... and then on Saturday, 9 May 2009, ironically, it rained.

The showerhead had become a fixture but there were many who felt it wasn't dignified and it wasn't fair to continue it on the new president. I even got a formal letter from that strange mouthful of an organisation – the Commission for the Promotion and Protection of the Rights of Cultural, Religious and Linguistic Communities – requesting that I reconsider. The pressure didn't bother me but I felt that I did need to mark the shift. I was deeply pessimistic about Zuma and angry with the ANC for choosing such a patently corrupt leader but, as a South African, I didn't want him to fail. I resolved the dilemma by using the showerhead as a sort of gauge. It would hover above his head to measure his probity and his actions. Knowing how much he loathed the showerhead, I even imagined how this semi-reprieve might goad him in some way into better behaviour. I held out a slim – but it was very slim – hope that the showerhead could, at some point, be removed completely.

ZAPIRO
Don't Mess With the President's Head

Cartoons from *Mail & Guardian*, *Sunday Times* and *The Times*

The early signs were promising. For a while Zuma seemed to be governing relatively well.

Not that there wasn't plenty of mud flying. Western Cape premier Helen Zille responded to criticism of her all-male cabinet by calling Zuma a womanising HIV-risk to his wives. The ANC Youth League and the MK Veterans spewed bile back about her cabinet being "sex boys to satisfy her well-evolved wild-whore libido".

The new minister of transport, Sbu Ndebele, received a R1m Merc and two cows from contractors who had done big business with his former provincial department and he saw no conflict of interest. He consulted the president after a media outcry.

Mbeki loyalists everywhere were being replaced by Zuma acolytes.

The snappily named Hawks were announced as the replacement for the Scorpions as a priority crime investigation unit. The Hawks predictably proved far less effective than the Scorpions and the Constitutional Court would later rule that the legislation which created them was invalid.

On his 91st birthday, the '67 Minutes for Mandela' campaign was launched. At the event Mandla Mandela claimed the icon's legacy for the family and the ANC, echoing Zuma's pre-election rebuff for the Nelson Mandela Foundation.

Early in his presidency Zuma received angry marchers at the Union Buildings and promised a clean-out of lazy councillors and an improvement in delivery.

In a remarkably positive moment, the president paid a surprise visit to Balfour in Mpumalanga and caught the mayor at home during office hours and publicly rebuked him.

Zuma has always played the religious card cleverly, seeking and gaining approval from various churches – even being proclaimed a pastor by some. Rhema Church head Ray McCauley led a conservative coalition of faith leaders which seemed to have the president's ear.

Just one year after Mbeki's removal there were rumours and conspiracy theories already running in the party about the future of the leadership and possible attempts to block Zuma from a second term.

Moe Shaik – brother of the corrupt Schabir and the sacked Arms Deal chief Chippy – had been humiliated by the Hefer Commission for attempting to smear Bulelani Ngcuka. He was damaged goods but he was an old ally of Zuma, so he became head of the SA Secret Service.

The language of debate within the ANC was getting increasingly savage. Malema had infamously said he would "kill for Zuma". The Youth League said prominent educationalist Professor Jonathan Jansen should be shot and killed for racism, and cabinet minister Fikile Mbalula said of alleged criminals that police should "shoot the bastards". Party veteran Kader Asmal commented: "We have lost our moral compass." The MK Veterans then told Asmal to go to the nearest cemetery and die.

Menzi Simelane has largely been forgotten in the tidal wave over the past decade of completely inappropriate appointees to public positions by Jacob Zuma but, for me, he was an early big red flag. He was so palpably compromised – found by a public inquiry to be a liar who had unlawfully engineered the axing of NPA head Vusi Pikoli. He also wasn't very clever in how he did his dirty work. Yet, simply because he was a blind loyalist who would do what he was told, Zuma made him director of the National Prosecuting Authority. Archbishop Desmond Tutu described the appointment as an "aberration" and three years later the Constitutional Court ruled him unfit for office.

Julius Malema had been a useful blunt instrument in Zuma's cause but he started to go off the song sheet and crudely attacked Tripartite Alliance partners.

Yet another baby bombshell. The president had fathered a child with the daughter of PSL soccer boss Irvin Khoza. More unprotected sex outside his three marriages – not what he had been preaching as government policy.

On the latest count, he now had 20 offspring although no one seemed to have an exact number and there were rumoured to be many more scattered through his trail of exile. At this point I put the showerhead firmly back in position. It was not about Zuma's morality or his traditional values and attitudes ... it was about his rampant hypocrisy and his behaviour being entirely at odds with what he was trotting out on public occasions.

This is one of my personal favourites of all my Zuma cartoons. I made it into a T-shirt which proved very popular but I was shocked to find that some people, who had enthusiastically bought the shirt, later confessed to being afraid to wear it in public.

He was forced by the party into a sort-of apology for his behaviour.

By SONA in February 2010, the nation was sniggering and horrified in equal measure by his behaviour.

Zuma attempted to pacify the increasingly troublesome Malema by talking up his leadership qualities.

In a moment which seemed to symbolise the newly aggressive state, a UCT student who flipped a finger at the president's convoy was accosted by bodyguards at gunpoint and roughed up. Later, Zuma's blue light bullies assaulted a grandmother and a photographer.

In March 2010, President Zuma paid a state visit to Britain.

Predictably, Zuma was mauled by the UK media and came home to face yet another personal crisis: after ten months in office he still had not declared his personal assets as required by law.

Malema had now become a major problem for Zuma. The ANC's disciplinary committee charged him with misconduct after he said that Zuma's criticism of the Youth League made him worse than Mbeki.

In a classic Zuma fudge, left-leaning economic development minister Ebrahim Patel and the more centrist Trevor Manuel at the National Planning Commission were left to battle it out over the fiscal future.

The increasingly surreal Zuma domestic soap opera took another turn. Media houses were sent allegations, possibly by Zuma family members, that his second wife Nompumelelo Ntuli-Zuma was pregnant with her bodyguard's child. The bodyguard had reportedly committed suicide seven months earlier. Several years later there would be claims that MaNtuli tried to poison her husband.

The government was pushing the Protection of Information Bill — a clumsy and heavy-handed piece of legislation that meant draconian prison sentences for publishing or even possessing info deemed classified on the arbitrary say-so of officials. They also wanted the press to be policed by a media tribunal answerable to parliament.

Zuma slammed the media for negativity and welcomed the ANC-aligned paper, *The New Age*, which was soon to be launched by his friends the Guptas.

Black Economic Empowerment was an important and necessary part of ANC policy but Zuma's family were blatantly privileged beneficiaries and were increasingly coming under the spotlight. His son Duduzane cleared R900m from an Arcelor-Mittal deal and his nephew Khulubuse amassed millions in DRC oil deals.

Zuma opened the ANC's National General Congress in Durban with a sharp dressing down of the Youth League and a warning on ill discipline, but he could not escape rampant speculation about his future.

Zuma's attitude to the media was summed up by the appointment of Mzwanele 'Jimmy' Manyi as his chief communicator. The Black Management Forum head was best known for bad relations with the press and for stirring racial controversy. Much later he would take titular ownership of the Gupta media assets when the brothers tried to cut some ties and cover some tracks.

THE LAST SUSHI
OCTOBER 2010–OCTOBER 2012

In 2010, the Gupta family seemed to be increasing their influence on Zuma all the time and were surfacing in media as the faces of cronyism. We had not yet heard the term 'State Capture'. The Guptas had arrived in South Africa from India in 1993 and built a business empire around Sahara Computers. They were adept at gaining government contracts and targeted Zuma and his family very early on as useful vehicles to help them expand their fortunes, mainly through a company called Oakbay Investments.

Cosatu's Zwelinzima Vavi had by now abandoned his support for Zuma and was highlighting the rampant corruption – using the word 'hyenas' to describe the beneficiaries.

Zapiro
The Last Sushi

Cartoons from *Mail & Guardian*, *Sunday Times* and *The Times*

Bling king and convicted criminal Kenny Kunene had ingratiated himself with the ANC Youth League. His notorious naked sushi birthday party, attended by Julius Malema, seemed to me to symbolise the moral abyss we were approaching.

Drawing the Guptas has always been difficult. I like to be accurate and make sure that I have every individual correctly identified and caricatured. But at this stage there weren't that many public images of them and the information was confusing. Rajesh is also known as Tony, Atul seems to be the oldest but isn't, and Ajay, whom we rarely see, is sometimes spoken of as AJ and sometimes as RJ. There are several nephews who appear in the mix now and then as well. In this cartoon I labelled Rajesh (Tony) and Ajay the wrong way round. To this day, the Guptas often get misidentified.

Zuma's handpicked police chief Bheki Cele had authorised a dodgy R500m lease for a police headquarters in Pretoria from a friend of Zuma's. The new public protector, Thuli Madonsela, a Zuma appointee, made herself famous by robustly condemning Cele for improper conduct in her report. She had laid down the first marker for her huge future role in the battle against State Capture.

Libyan leader Muammar Gaddafi was another big problem for Zuma. The rogue North African leader was attacking his own people and South Africa hesitantly voted in favour of a UN Security Council resolution which enabled NATO air strikes against him. But Gaddafi had been a generous funder of the ANC and reportedly had also bankrolled Zuma's fightback campaign after Mbeki isolated him. Zuma made at least one personal trip to Tripoli in that time. And South Africa had also provided some of the arms that Gaddafi was using in the civil war.

The 2011 local government elections gave the ANC a jolt. The DA, led by Helen Zille, cemented its grip across the Western Cape and significantly grew national support.

In a shocking episode, not condemned by the party, ANC Eastern Cape regional leader Nceba Faku incited his followers to burn down the offices of the Port Elizabeth newspaper which had exposed his involvement in tender fraud. I gave Lady Justice a twin sister.

Then the government started to railroad the Protection of Information Bill (dubbed the Secrecy Bill) through parliament and pressed ahead with old plans for a media tribunal.

The Arms Deal just would not go away. Swedish company SAAB outed its UK partner BAE for paying huge 'bonuses' to its South African consultant Fana Hlongwane.

The new evidence prompted Hawks head Anwar Dramat to make further inquiries.

A classic Zuma cock-up. Almost every legal expert said the extension of Chief Justice Sandile Ngcobo's term needed to be re-worked to be constitutionally valid. His lawyers ignored the clamour and the respected judge felt obliged to withdraw before the deadline expired and he was lost to the court.

To replace Ngcobo, Zuma deliberately overlooked the independence and exceptional qualifications of Deputy Chief Justice Dikgang Moseneke. He opted instead for Mogoeng Mogoeng, a former apartheid homeland judge and an evangelical conservative with a track record of sexism and homophobia. I was soon calling him Moegoe Moegoe.

Mogoeng Mogoeng went on to surprise Zuma, most observers and me with a robust track record of brave rulings against both the president and the government. Which makes this cartoon look unfair and misplaced in hindsight. That is the daily cartoonist's lot. This is the way it appeared to me at the time and it felt entirely valid.

The Malema issue had careered out of control. When the ANC held a disciplinary hearing against him at Luthuli House, his supporters rioted outside and burned Zuma T-shirts.

Under pressure from a looming court ruling, Zuma reluctantly announced the establishment of an inquiry into the Arms Deal. At the time, this was greeted with celebration but the Seriti Commission was limited by its cynically narrow terms of reference and even narrower mindset and proved to be an expensive waste of time and money.

Parliament voted on the Secrecy Bill. The date of the vote was shifted from a Wednesday deliberately to avoid obvious links to Black Wednesday in 1977 when the apartheid government launched a massive crackdown on independent media voices and closed *The World* newspaper.

Another Zuma appointment went disastrously awry when the brand-new Special Investigating Unit head Willem Heath resigned after making a libellous claim that Thabo Mbeki had orchestrated the rape and corruption charges against Zuma.

Malema had been suspended by the party. One weekend I woke up to find a huge picture of him on the front of the *Sunday Times* with a hand above his head imitating my showerhead as a way of getting at Zuma. Then on TV I saw him leading supporters, who were all doing the same gesture, in singing "the shower man is giving us trouble".

Malema had played a key role in Mbeki's downfall in 2008. Now he extolled the virtues of Mbeki in contrast to Zuma.

The ANC disciplinary process against Malema dragged on. The party heavies couldn't decide whether his suspension should start immediately or after a mitigation hearing.

Finally they acted.

Pravin Gordhan was labouring away as finance minister, trying to make sense and economic viability out of Zuma's promises and poor fiscal discipline.

On 8 January 2012, the ANC celebrated its centenary but everyone was already far more focused on the first elective conference since the Polokwane chaos, which was scheduled for Mangaung in the Free State in December.

The ANC shared its centenary with one of the world's most famous disasters.

Zuma copped a legal setback in March 2012 when the Appeal Court ordered the NPA to hand over to the DA records of material considered in the decision to drop the fraud and corruption charges.

For me this cartoon is emblematic of Zuma's entire public life – I imagined him rattling around in the Union Buildings at night hearing sounds and being haunted by the thought that his nefarious past would one day catch up with him.

Crime intelligence boss Richard Mdluli was a key shady figure at this time. As he was seen as a Zuma ally, a series of serious charges against him and investigations into his behaviour were all either dropped or postponed. He was rumoured to be the man who leaked the spy tapes to Zuma's legal team; he was charged with murder and kidnapping; he was publicly accused of tapping cabinet ministers' phones; he allegedly looted department funds. He also seemed to have the dirt on everyone or to know where to find it. Outrageously, he remained on full pay (albeit with many years on suspension) until after Zuma's downfall in 2018.

In foreign policy terms, the BRICS were a big deal for Jacob Zuma. The top guns in the developing world had invited us to their table.

Fathers' Day 2012

In May 2012, artist Brett Murray exhibited his now notorious painting 'The Spear' at the Goodman Gallery in Johannesburg. The reaction was furious and dangerous.

Brett and I are old friends. I am not sure what Rondebosch Boys High did to produce two such troublemakers in quick succession. He was two years behind me at the school.

The ANC launched a defamation suit and bullied the gallery into taking down the painting (which was also defaced by two protesters – actions which were caught on camera) and they also forced *City Press* editor Ferial Haffajee to remove imagery of the painting from the paper's website. Brett had to go into hiding and we watched the televised court proceedings against him together. It was a really nasty time for anyone defending freedom of speech and artistic expression.

OCTOBER 2010–OCTOBER 2012

In the midst of the suit against Brett, my lawyers and I had been busy preparing our defence for Zuma's legal action against me regarding the Rape of Lady Justice cartoon. It had been pending for four years and was now finally due to go to court. Not knowing whether the case would actually go ahead, I thought of a cover for my 2012 annual that would work whichever way things went.

The case against me was withdrawn at the 11th hour. We believed that Zuma's lawyers and some ANC heavies had for some time been urging him to drop the proceedings, especially given the likely embarrassment in the run-up to Mangaung, but the president had stubbornly wanted to go ahead. I presume he was finally persuaded that his evidence under oath in defence of his own dignity would have been excruciating and compromising. And we had assembled formidable evidence of the number of times the figures depicted in the cartoon had threatened the legal system in some way.

After the charges were dropped, Mac Maharaj, Zuma's spokesperson, repeated all the original slurs against me in the suit and then laughably claimed that the charges had been dropped to promote free speech.

This legal failure soon caused the Zuma defamation dam to burst — he dropped all his remaining defamation suits against media, including the 2006 case against me for the three cartoons about his rape trial.

Kgalema Motlanthe was assumed to be running against Zuma at Mangaung but his candidacy was undeclared. Much Byzantine importance was placed on the economic policy distinction between Zuma's championing of 'the Second Transition' as against 'the Second Phase of the Transition' mooted by his opponents.

OCTOBER 2010–OCTOBER 2012 | 127

The Second Transition clearly included a massively expensive new presidential jet.

Marikana was a horrifying and defining moment: 34 striking mineworkers shot dead by police. Julius Malema was first on the scene slamming police, mine bosses, fat cat unionists and Zuma.

Zuma's response was clumsy and slow. Eventually he tried to assert himself.

Zuma appointed retired judge Ian Farlam to investigate the massacre.

Spiralling strikes and protests in the wake of Marikana were met with a typical blame shift.

More miners vented their anger, transport strikers torched buses. An air of chaos prevailed as the party went through preparatory processes for the Mangaung conference.

NUMBER ONE
OCTOBER 2012–OCTOBER 2013

Nkandla was a word we were starting to hear a lot more. The expensive development of Zuma's rural base in KZN cropped up in the Schabir Shaik trial way back in 2005 but it was only when details of exorbitant state expenditure on his private residence – as much as R200m on first reports – started to appear that it became a byword for the abuse of taxpayers' money. Farcically, the government tried to keep the spending a secret on the grounds that Nkandla was a national key point but Thuli Madonsela, with public support, was having none of that.

Cyril Ramaphosa was now back in politics and tipped to become Zuma's party deputy at Mangaung. He was a director and shareholder of Lonmin, the company which owned the Marikana mine. An e-mail he wrote before the Marikana shootings painted him as a hard mine boss urging tough actions against strikers.

I was deeply sceptical about the role Ramaphosa could play as deputy president in the Zuma kleptocracy and what he might one day inherit.

At a talk shortly after this cartoon was published, I wondered aloud whether the old Cyril from activist days, whom I had admired, would ever again emerge. As I signed books afterwards, someone asked me to sign one for "Cyril". I said "Do you mean Cyril Cyril?" She said yes, so I wrote in the book "For Cyril, hoping the old Cyril is still in there somewhere".

Protecting the president had become an obsession. SACP boss Blade Nzimande supported a call for a new law which would forbid any derogatory comments about Zuma.

Pressed on the issue of public funds being wasted on Nkandla, Zuma told parliament that he had a bond. Maharaj said proof of the bond would be provided but not made public.

An auditors' report, buried when his corruption case was dropped, revealed millions of rands in payments to Zuma from many benefactors including Nelson Mandela.

Zuma crushed his only opponent, Kgalema Motlanthe, at Mangaung. Ramaphosa, an embarrassingly rich man, was now deputy president and had to dispose of, or ring-fence, any potentially conflicting assets.

Public works minister Thulas Nxesi reported that a total of R206m was spent on 'security upgrades' at Nkandla yet there was no public spending on Zuma's private home.

The Guptas had secretly funded the ANC. Their newspaper *The New Age* had very few readers and no credibility yet it got extraordinary financial support from the state in the form of advertising and funding for business breakfasts, which the SABC broadcast for free.

The Guptas announced that they would expand into television news as well.

Thirteen SA support troops were killed while defending the dodgy leader of the Central African Republic (CAR). As Zuma hosted the 2013 BRICS summit in Durban, the *Mail & Guardian* revealed that the troops were probably there to protect mining interests linked to ANC politicians.

The president accused the *M&G* of "pissing on the graves of gallant fighters".

Cosatu general secretary Zwelinzima Vavi, the main Tripartite Alliance critic of corruption, was accused of corruption himself in connection with the purchase of new union premises. It looked like a purge attempt by Cosatu chairman Sdumo Dlamini and other Zuma allies. Vavi's case was not helped by a subsequent sexual scandal.

The Guptas truly exploded into the headlines in May 2013. Atul Gupta's niece was getting married at Sun City in an extravagant affair with Zuma invited as the guest of honour. In an extraordinary breach of security and protocol, a commercial jet carrying guests flew from India directly into Waterkloof military base, bypassing customs and getting a VIP government welcome. There was an immediate outcry and Zuma decided not to go to Sun City. In later years, attendance at this wedding would become a mark of shame for many, including a senior KPMG partner implicated in auditing failures. And in later years it would also become clear that the South African taxpayer had footed the huge bill for the occasion through corrupt, disguised payments.

For almost the first time, senior party figures expressed anger at Gupta influence but, officially, the blame for the blatant abuse of state facilities was pinned solely on the Indian high commissioner and two lowly functionaries.

I reflected the extent of the Guptas' pervasive influence by coining the expression Guptastan when I did a cartoon on the return home of 77-year-old Dr Cyril Karabus after nine months of entirely unwarranted imprisonment in the UAE.

A Guptastan YouTube meme soon surfaced and went wild.

Zuma signed the unpopular e-tolling bill into law, provoking a major collision with the trade unions and with civil action groups.

By now we had seen footage of another distinctive Zuma foible — the rather unfortunate use of his middle finger to push up his glasses.

There were yet more legal troubles for Zuma when the High Court ordered the NPA to hand over to the DA the previously secret spy tapes, which the NPA had used as the basis for dropping charges against Zuma.

As expected, his state-funded lawyers appealed the court's decision, an action which produced one of my darkest cartoons.

Richard Calland, a leading political analyst, sparked an angry response from the ANC when he remarked about Zuma: "It's not that he can't read, it's that he doesn't read and he doesn't read the proper stuff; he doesn't read cabinet briefs, he doesn't read stuff that is the meat and drink of modern, sophisticated government."

An affidavit from one of the fall guys in the Gupta Waterkloof airport scandal confirmed what everyone knew – that Zuma was the "number one" referred to in a Justice Department report as the person who gave the go-ahead for the Gupta plane to use the defence force facility.

Zuma played the religious card again when he told a Limpopo evangelical congregation that God had made a connection between government and the church and that they should pray for the government.

THE CHICKEN RUN
OCTOBER 2013–MARCH 2015

The sums involved in the Nkandla upgrade were mind-boggling. This was such a blatant rip-off. Equally blatant, and desperate, were the state's attempts to avoid scrutiny.

Public protector Thuli Madonsela had submitted a report and the government was determined it should remain secret. They interdicted her for 'breaching state security'. After this cartoon was published, someone referenced *The Lord of the Rings* with a post: "Go Gandalf the Grey".

The cabinet was forced to back down from its legal challenge.

The saga got weirder when two security ministers claimed it was illegal for the media to take and publish any photos of the sprawling Nkandla site.

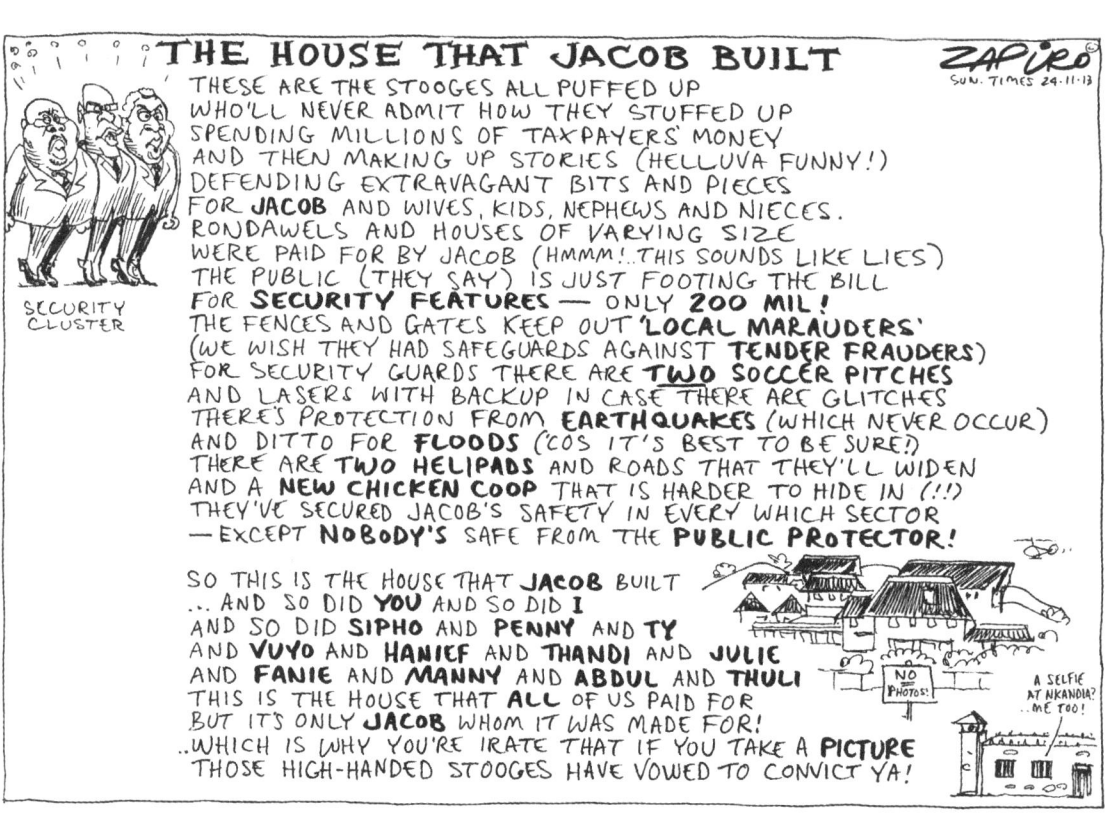

R2.8m was spent on a swimming pool which would later be officially justified as a 'fire pool' for extinguishing blazes on thatched roofs.

On 5 December 2013 Nelson Mandela passed away. There was a public viewing of his body at the Union Buildings.

At the Mandela memorial service at Soccer City, President Obama delivered soaring oratory while Zuma was roundly booed by sections of the crowd. Obama was given a signed copy of this cartoon at a dinner in Washington and sent me a handwritten note of thanks for it. Apparently he didn't ever do e-mails for that kind of task.

THE WHITE HOUSE
WASHINGTON

Jonathan —
Thanks for the wonderful cartoon. Mandela's funeral remains one of seminal memories of my presidency.
Best wishes,

There was a media sensation over the use of an unqualified interpreter for the deaf who had not been given a security screening.

SONA in February 2014 was meant to mark 20 years of democracy but it was marked more by security fears that Zuma would be embarrassed.

Zuma's attempt to position his own presidency in some sort of historical context was jaw-droppingly devoid of self-awareness.

I was busy at the time with the cover for my 20-year commemorative book *DemoCrazy* on which the admirable but short-term Kgalema Motlanthe only made it onto the back.

Thuli Madonsela also had Hlaudi Motsoeneng in her sights. The SABC boss was a prime example of Zuma's appalling appointments on loyalty rather than legality or ability. Motsoeneng survived a litany of misdemeanours that should have felled him simply because, as the incompetent communications minister Faith Muthambi once said, "Baba loves him, he loves him so much."

After facing down multiple official attempts to block her, the public protector finally got to release her report on Nkandla. She found that Zuma and his family improperly benefited from the upgrades, he had violated the Ethics Code and that he must pay back some of the money.

Her damning report gave the lie to expensive features like a new chicken run being classified as essential security upgrades. Her report also compromised the security cluster ministers who had been shamelessly defending the spending.

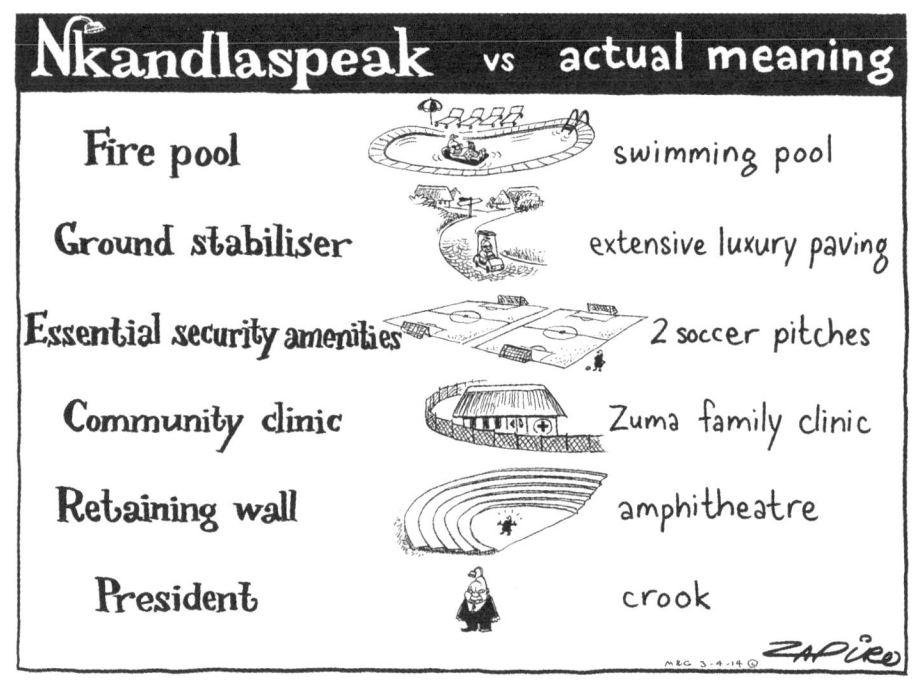

When I did this cartoon I originally had the word 'thief' in the bottom line. *The Mail & Guardian* said they loved the cartoon but their lawyers were concerned about that word 'thief'. After a bit of back and forth I asked if the word 'crook' would be OK. They went back to the lawyers who said crook would be fine, which I thought was hilarious. On the same day, after I'd filed my cartoon and too late for changes, the High Court ruled that a DA text message, "How Zuma stole your money", was fair comment because of the phrase "licence to loot" in Madonsela's report.

So I then did this cartoon for the *Sunday Times*. And this time the lawyers (the same ones consulted by the *M&G*) gave 'thief' the go-ahead. Funnier still!

On Freedom Day 2014, with the 2014 election looming, the Arch announced with a heavy heart that he could no longer support the ANC.

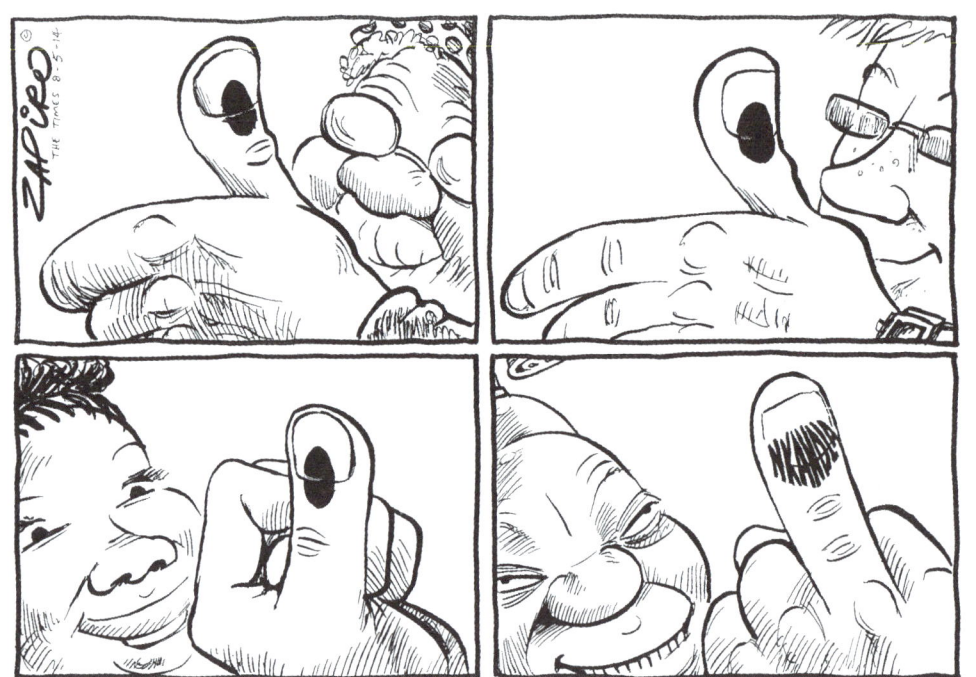

There were some warning signs for the ANC in the details of the polling results but, in spite of everything Zuma had inflicted on the nation, the party still got 60% of the popular vote.

There was to be one big change in parliament. Julius Malema's Economic Freedom Fighters had got a million votes and 25 MPs who were not going to play by the old decorous rules of the house.

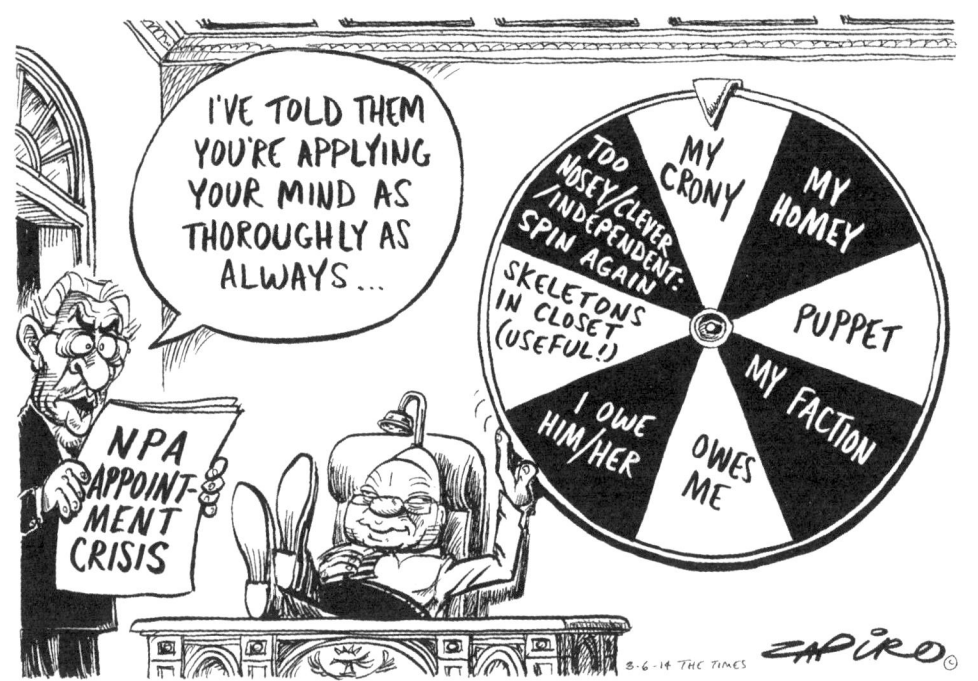

Returned to office, Zuma promptly botched another official appointment. His latest choice to run the NPA, and to keep him out of court, was Mxolisi Nxasana, who had failed to get security clearance because he hadn't declared an old murder charge.

Nepotism went to the next level when the president's daughter Thuthukile was made the youngest-ever head of a minister's office at the age of 25.

The Special Investigating Unit belatedly rumbled into action on the Nkandla overspending and went after the architect Minenhle Makhanya while ignoring everyone else.

After fighting for years, the president's lawyers conceded in court that they had no legal grounds for blocking the DA's access to the spy tapes.

#PayBackTheMoney took off on social media with a lot of amplification from the EFF, even though, somewhat ironically, Julius Malema was also under pressure to pay the taxman a big debt.

Thuli criticised Zuma's response to the Nkandla report and repeated her demand that he repay some of the money. The ANC replied that she was overstepping her powers and dictating to the legislature.

Hard though it was to believe now, Madonsela had been one of Zuma's first appointments in 2009.

As always, Zuma was obsessed with the intelligence services. He purged three top spies.

The Dalai Lama wanted to attend a summit of Nobel Peace laureates in Cape Town. To please their Chinese masters, our government denied him a visa — and not for the first time. The summit was cancelled in protest.

The president's nephew Khulubuse Zuma was now the poster child of political enrichment. He had made millions (possibly billions) in a disgraced mining venture and thousands attended his extravagant Nkandla nuptials to a Swazi princess, who was one of his four fiancées at the time. This cartoon references a famous work 'Gargantua' by the 19th-century French caricaturist and artist Honoré Daumier.

The *Sunday Times* reported that Zuma had accepted a bribe from a French arms company in 2000 by using the code words "I see the Eiffel Tower lights are shining today".

OCTOBER 2013–MARCH 2015 | 165

Zuma saddled Deputy President Ramaphosa with just about every tough or smelly task, one of which was getting parties working together again to restore a functional parliament.

The president refused to face up to parliamentary questions on Nkandla. By now, I, and many others, were picking up on his jarring habit of chuckling "Heh Heh Heh" in the most inappropriate of circumstances.

2014 had felt pretty catastrophic and SONA 2015, which was held at a time of hectic Eskom load shedding, made me think things were only going to get worse.

The event descended into chaos. Mystery devices jammed cell phone signals. Plainclothes cops, dressed as waiters, violently evicted EFF members. Zuma just giggled and delivered a reality-free speech in typically stilted mode.

During another speech, Zuma mused, "If I were a dictator I would change a few things …"

RESERVOIR DOGS
MAY 2015–FEBRUARY 2016

Zuma's scheme was clearly to make the NPA dysfunctional. He wanted the new head Mxolisi Nxasana out but Nxasana fought for his job and accused top lieutenants like Nomgcobo Jiba of using state resources to dig up dirt on him.

Two cabinet ministers produced an unintentionally comical video (with the added insanity of 'O Sole Mio' as a soundtrack!) showing that everything at Nkandla was essential for security including the fire pool, that Zuma owed nothing and ... even more must be spent to maintain standards.

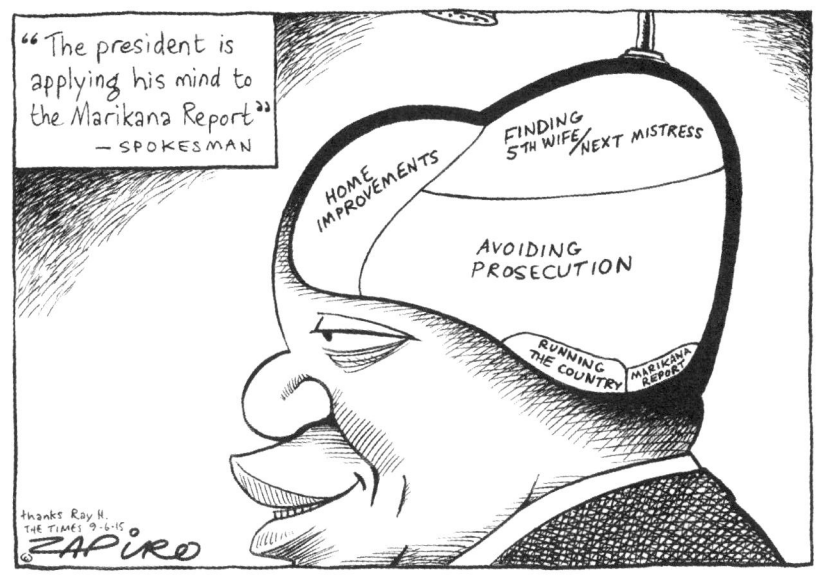

The Marikana disaster was completely unresolved. Judge Farlam had handed over his report into the massacre to the president three months before and still there was no action from him.

Finally, the report was made public ... on the anniversary of the ANC's most famous proclamation of democracy .... and, no surprise, the politicians escaped unscathed.

At last there was a split in the senior ranks. ANC Gauteng chair Paul Mashatile became the first party heavyweight to publicly distance himself from the Nkandla spending.

The government brazenly flouted a Pretoria court order and colluded in the departure from South Africa of Sudanese President al-Bashir, wanted by the International Criminal Court for Darfur war crimes.

MAY 2015–FEBRUARY 2016 | 173

A Soshanguve pastor was exposed for feeding snakes to his followers in the name of their salvation. This seemed to me to be an appropriate metaphor for Zuma foisting on us the exorbitantly expensive nuclear power deal which he wanted to make with his Russian pals. There was an assumption that there were lucrative kickbacks being lined up. This issue would dog us until Zuma's departure, when the nuclear deal was quietly buried.

The ANC Women's League were horrendously compromised by their loyalty to Zuma. His sexism and his scandals drew no criticism from their lips.

Zuma found another lackey to run the NPA in the form of Shaun Abrahams, later to find notoriety among cartoonists as Shaun the Sheep for his slavish performance (or non-performance) of his duties. Among his first acts was to withdraw charges against his discredited deputy, Nomgcobo Jiba. She was another Zuma loyalist who faced serious allegations of perjury and fraud and would later be struck off the roll.

Having hand-picked Mogoeng Mogoeng as the new chief justice, Zuma did not get what he expected. First the judge confronted the president on political intimidation of the courts. Then he would go on to deliver or oversee a sequence of powerfully independent judgments.

The appointment of Mosebenzi Zwane as mining minister was pivotal. The Guptas had significant mining interests and clearly had put their man in place to do their bidding. Zwane was completely unqualified for the task and had no serious political credentials. It was a transparent piece of State Capture. But it was also an over-reach. From that moment, the hand of the Guptas would be suspected everywhere.

During parliamentary questions Zuma said: "I don't know how to stop my laughter. Is it hurting? No."

Possibly the defining moment of Zuma's presidency came on 9 December 2015 when he suddenly fired respected finance minister Nhlanhla Nene and replaced him with the neophyte, Gupta-linked Des van Rooyen. Officially the reason was that Nene was moving to a BRICS job (which, of course, never materialised) but everyone knew that Nene was blocking the dodgy dealings of a Zuma favourite and rumoured girlfriend, South African Airways chair Dudu Myeni. Nene was trying to maintain our fiscal credibility as the possibility of a sub-investment level rating for our national debt loomed for the first time. Everyone also knew that Zuma and the Guptas were frustrated by their inability to get Nene and the finance ministry to do their bidding.

After Nene's axing, the rand plummeted. The president was forced into a humiliating retreat by intense pressure from a combination of party heavyweights and business leaders. After only four days in the job, 'Weekend Special' Van Rooyen was shunted off to another cabinet position and Pravin Gordhan returned to the finance ministry with a guaranteed free hand to deal with SAA and other wayward state-owned enterprises.

Opposition to Zuma was now out in the open and he was criticised from all sides. 2015 ended with protest marches in several cities.

2016 began with Zuma being quick as ever to find a distracting target. He and his government responded to a racist rant from retired KZN estate agent Penny Sparrow with threats of heavy-handed government action.

Investors and ratings agencies had been rattled by the Nene firing. At the 2016 World Economic Forum in Davos, Gordhan did his best to restore matters.

It was no secret that Zuma resented having Gordhan foisted on him and he had a key ally in Tom Moyane, the head of SARS who was destroying the hard-won reputation of that agency and did not appreciate Pravin's Mr Clean approach to things. Nor did he like reporting to him. Moyane was dishing dirt on Gordhan through a KPMG report into an alleged rogue unit at SARS in the days when Gordhan ran it. This report would later be thoroughly discredited but, at the time, the Sunday Times was giving unwarranted credence to it with a series of reports. I learned from respected journalists like Marianne Thamm (of Daily Maverick) and Pearlie Joubert the true state of affairs and produced this cartoon for The Times – the sister paper of the Sunday Times. Clearly it ran against what the group was reporting. There was a sequence of very awkward conversations in which the editor suggested removing the KPMG report from the cartoon – which would make the whole thing meaningless. I refused and they reluctantly ran the cartoon unchanged. I have since wondered whether this exchange was a factor in my subsequently deteriorating relationship with the Sunday Times, which ended after twenty years in 2018.

More evidence was now emerging of Gupta influence in cabinet appointments, the party was speaking out against State Capture and Pravin was nobly trying to cut costs.

Faced with an inevitable defeat in the highest court, in a case brought by opposition parties, Zuma ended years of defiance of the public protector in February 2016 and agreed to #PayBackTheMoney for the illegal Nkandla upgrades.

The president's case had taken an absolute hammering in court and his highly paid legal counsel had advised an almost complete surrender.

Zuma's sudden acceptance of his legal obligations threw his blindly loyal comrades under the bus including ministers Nathi Mthethwa and Thulas Nxesi, and speaker Baleka Mbete.

SONA had become an annual ordeal for Zuma and 2016 was no different. DA leader Mmusi Maimane said he lived on Planet Zuma; Malema called him an illegitimate president and began using the catchy word 'Zuptas' to describe the State Capture cabal.

ANC secretary general Gwede Mantashe seriously suggested that he had evidence of meetings at the American embassy designed to mobilise opposition and plant seeds of anarchy.

The 2016 budget speech was seen as the most important since democratic government was established. The pressure was on Pravin to avert a ratings downgrade. Which, somehow, he managed to do.

DEAD PRESIDENT WALKING
MARCH 2016–FEBRUARY 2017

The finance minister was now the media's hero (excepting the Gupta mouthpieces and state media). The credibility of the government rested on him. A resentful Zuma and his lieutenant Tom Moyane continued to target him through a Hawks investigation but this time Gordhan was not alone.

Deputy finance minister Mcebisi Jonas revealed that the Guptas offered him the finance minister's job (and a R600m enticement!) weeks before Nhlanhla Nene was sacked. Jonas said he had turned them down.

I think this cartoon was my definitive statement about the Guptas and State Capture. It appeared on the front page of the *Mail & Guardian*.

High drama when the Constitutional Court unanimously ruled that the president was bound to comply with Thuli's Nkandla report and said that he had violated the constitution and his oath of office. (At this time, for a short period only, Thuli radically changed her hairstyle. That's always frustrating for a cartoonist because we have to adjust our drawings. In this case, it worked in my favour because her new look made for a perfect gavel head.)

Surely no politician in a democracy could survive such a stinging and serious rebuke?

The original *Sunday Times* cartoon, which was the basis for this annual book cover, included a small icon (above) which sparked some hilarity online.

But somehow the oaf would cling on to office for another 20 months ... starting with a televised address in which he said sorry (sort of) and declined to resign. Deliberately, that appearance was made late on a Friday night when he assumed few would be watching. Worse still, Gwede Mantashe said the party would not request him to resign.

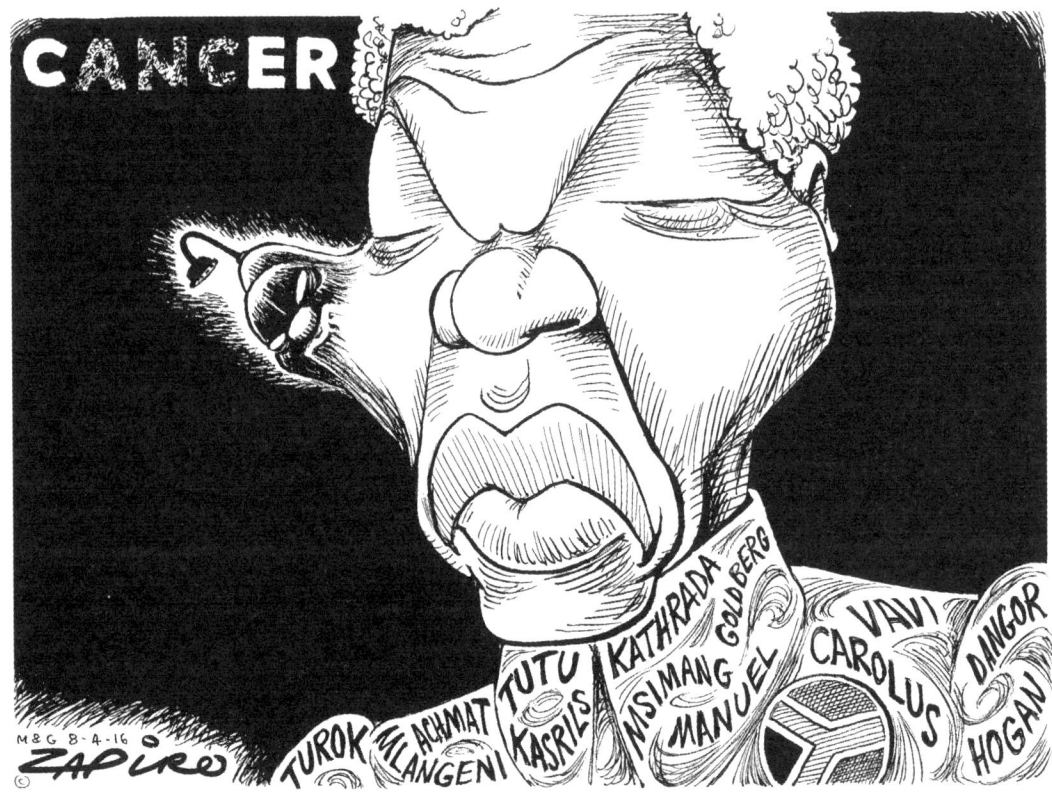

The alliance that railroaded Zuma's trip to power was now well and truly fractured. It was time to revisit that controversial cartoon from a decade ago.

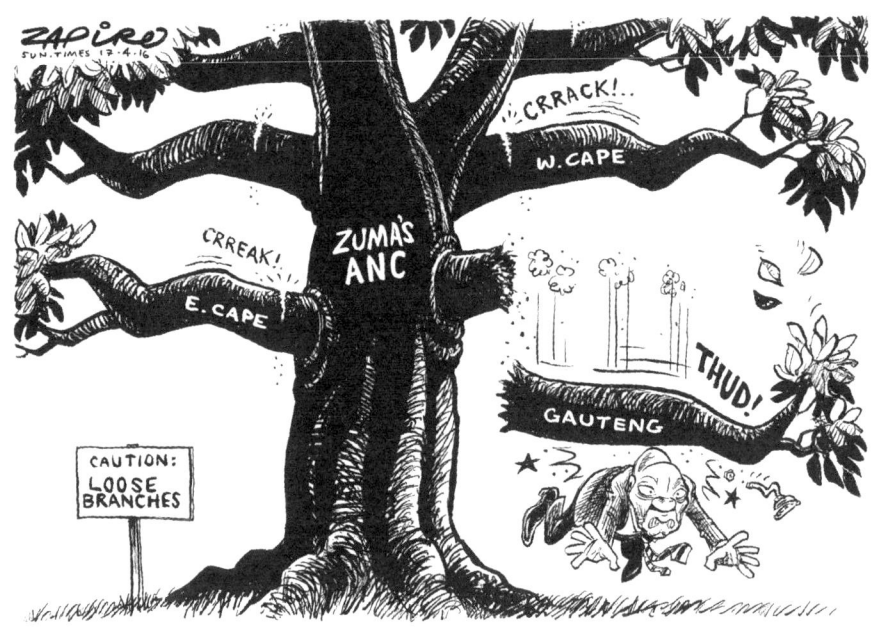

Not everyone in the ANC was buying what Zuma was selling. The Sefako Nyaka branch of the party in Gauteng called on him to resign or face disciplinary action. And some top brass were reported to be seeking his departure.

One constant source of resentment was the obscene cost of state support for Zuma's many wives. A cabinet minister revealed a staggering bill for their top-end cars.

The ANC had launched an inquiry into State Capture but Gwede Mantashe scrapped it after only one person put a submission in writing.

As usual, Thuli Madonsela was prepared to go where others feared to tread. With only a few months left in office, she began a vigorous probe.

The 2016 local election campaign was well under way. DA adverts used Mandela quotes which sparked petty squabbles over his spiritual inheritance.

The local elections saw the usual poster clutter on lampposts. Even though it was a local election most of the parties insisted on using their national leaders' images rather than the councillors we would actually be voting for. The image used by the ANC of Zuma's head was so large that it almost filled the poster and, when attached to the poles, looked very much like my signature way of portraying him, something that was widely noticed on social media.

The elections saw major setbacks for the ANC with the unprecedented loss of control of Johannesburg, Pretoria and Port Elizabeth, where soccer boss Danny Jordaan had been wheeled in as mayor to try and save the day.

During the campaign Zuma had repeated his claim that "the ANC will fully rule until Jesus Christ returns".

In a powerful silent protest, three women marked the 10th anniversary of Zuma's acquittal on rape charges by bravely standing in front of him with placards calling out the accuser Khwezi's name. Senior ANC women responded with outrage at their "disrespect".

Zuma's supporters had so severely harassed Khwezi that she had fled to Europe for some years. Just two months after the Women's Day protest, Khwezi died aged 42.

A letter from the Hawks implied that Pravin Gordhan was now a suspect and could be arrested. The mind boggled that Gordhan could be targeted when he was the main guy trying to clean the stables.

This cartoon generated the biggest online response I've ever received ... by far. Previously a cartoon of mine had been seen 600,000 times on Facebook. This one got 2.25m views.

One upside in all of this was that the Guptas had become radioactive in business terms. No one would deal with them, including the banks. In September 2016 they announced that they were selling some of their South African shareholdings.

MARCH 2016–FEBRUARY 2017 | 199

In a surprise announcement, Zuma said he had paid R7.8m owed on Nkandla upgrades, complying with the Constitutional Court ruling. It was just a fraction of the R250m spent on the place and there were serious questions about where he got the money for the repayment from. It would turn out to be from the small-scale VBS Mutual Bank, which in 2018 collapsed in an abyss of mismanagement.

A desperate hunt for missing zama zamas (illegal miners) trapped underground in Gauteng gave me an opportunity to draw the full cast of the main State Capture characters in one place. Several more would be added to this lot before Zuma's time was up.

One of Zuma's biggest cronies, Vivian Reddy, initiated a *crimen injuria* action because of his appearance in this cartoon. Of course the case never went anywhere but I found it highly amusing that Reddy seemed prepared to throw his son under the bus in his complaint by pointing to him as the person who should be in the cartoon!

Halloween 2016 provided another opportunity to round up the villains.

The Hawks never did come for Gordhan but the NPA laid trumped-up charges against him at the very time he had a difficult medium-term budget statement to deliver.

In an obvious charade, Zuma said Gordhan was innocent until proven guilty and the law must be allowed to take its course.

Then Abrahams had to backpedal humiliatingly, finding on review that Gordhan "did not have the requisite intention to act unlawfully" and withdrawing the charges.

The Pretoria High Court ordered the public protector's report 'State of Capture' to be released. The state had interdicted, obstructed and obfuscated on the report but now we got to see 355 pages of damning evidence which implicated Zuma and family members, some ministers and parastatal execs, and the main players — brothers Ajay, Atul and Rajesh Gupta. Madonsela recommended that Zuma appoint a commission of inquiry headed by a judge solely selected by the chief justice.

Eskom CEO and former head of Transnet, Brian Molefe, had now become a key State Capture figure ... and a figure of fun. Thuli's report tied him to the Gupta mansion in Saxonwold through traced cell phone records. Bizarrely, Molefe claimed that those might have been visits to a mysterious shebeen in the upmarket area. No journalist could find a shebeen anywhere in Saxonwold. Molefe tearfully resigned from Eskom although he would later claim that it was in fact 'early retirement' in order to justify a whopping R30m payout. And Molefe would still have his uses for the Zuptas.

In spite of the overwhelming evidence, the ANC still did not move against Zuma. There were some divisions reported from an NEC meeting but no actions were taken.

Time for me to wheel out the Humpty-Dumpty metaphor yet again.

Donald Trump's bewildering election as president of the United States was greeted in South Africa with a degree of "maybe we don't have the worst president in the world" relief. Before he was inaugurated there were explosive, unverified allegations that the Russians had some dirt on Trump about strange sexual preferences. When this cartoon was published, Trevor Noah said he had bet his colleagues on The Daily Show in New York that I would draw Trump this way. For once I didn't mind being predictable.

Noah would soon be hailed as one of the world's next-generation leaders and he cracked a famous magazine cover.

What became known as the Life Esidimeni scandal rocked the nation. 94 mentally ill patients had died in Gauteng after being transferred to unlicensed facilities. Officials failed to take responsibility and Zuma failed to respond appropriately.

He also proceeded with a characteristically disengaged SONA 2017 speech that once again followed the EFF's violent removal from parliament and the DA's walkout.

THE SAXONWOLD SHEBEEN
FEBRUARY 2017–DECEMBER 2017

Disgraced former Eskom CEO Brian Molefe was hastily deployed to parliament as an MP just before the 2017 budget day. It was widely assumed, and reported, that he was being lined up to take Pravin Gordhan's job in an obvious move to capture the Treasury.

Social development minister Bathabile Dlamini was an appalling cabinet minister. She defied the Constitutional Court and placed 11 million grant recipients at risk over an illegal contract. This was a looming catastrophe spotlighted by NGOs and media. Parliament and the courts got involved. Zuma defiantly protected her because she protected him as a shameful leader of the ANC Women's League.

Another atrocious Zuma appointee was Major General Berning Ntlemeza. A former apartheid-era cop, he was the latest in a succession of Hawks heads and was patently unfit for office except for his reported allegiance to both Zuma and suspended police intelligence chief Richard Mdluli. He had led the pursuit of Gordhan. Following the latest brutal slap-down from the High Court, Ntlemeza headed for church.

Zuma had run out of patience ... or maybe the Guptas had. Pravin was on an international investment roadshow and his deputy Mcebisi Jonas was about to join him. Suddenly Zuma cancelled the trip and ordered Gordhan home. The rand plummeted. It seemed incomprehensible that he would brazenly repeat the utter disaster of Nene's sacking, but what other reason could there be for the recall?

Struggle legend Ahmed Kathrada died and Zuma stayed away from the funeral in accordance with the family's wishes. In his eulogy, former president Kgalema Motlanthe quoted Kathy's open letter, written a year earlier, calling on Zuma to stand down.

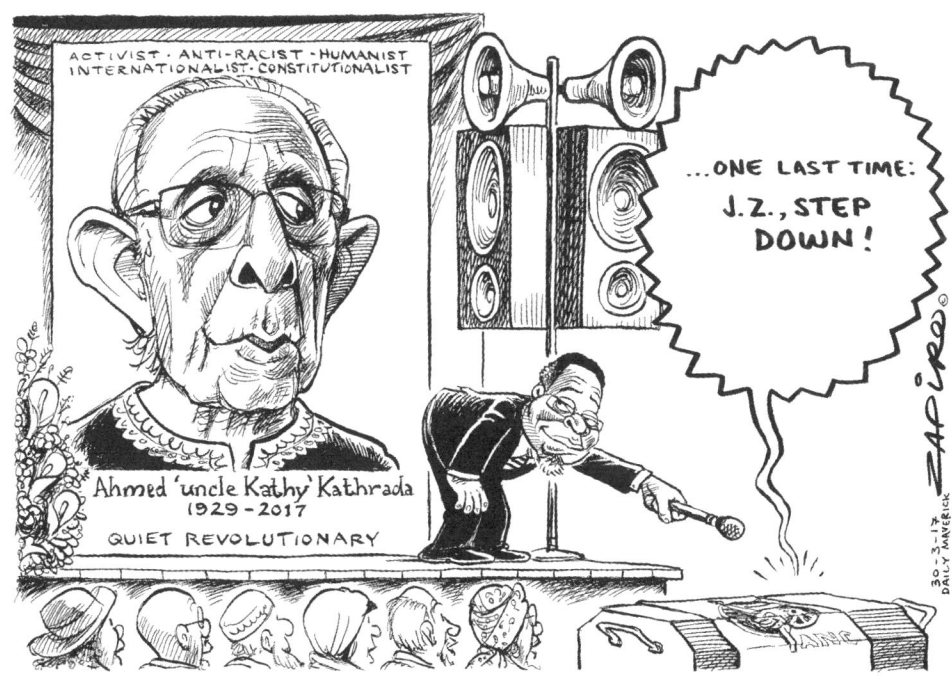

Well versed in the dark arts, Zuma again moved in the dead of night. He proclaimed the need for radical economic transformation and replaced Gordhan, not with Brian Molefe, as many had expected, but with another Gupta-linked figure in Malusi Gigaba.

Just four days after Gordhan's axing, the Standard & Poor's ratings agency downgraded our credit to the long-dreaded sub-investment levels.

Three of the ANC's top six, including secretary general Gwede Mantashe, criticised the reshuffle and then backed down in a National Working Committee meeting.

Mantashe said Zuma's critics within the party should not air their views in public. This spineless statement coincided with Easter.

Over 100,000 people attended an anti-Zuma protest at the Union Buildings. This cartoon is a re-working of a classic by the late, great Derek Bauer, who penned it for the *Weekly Mail* in 1989 in reference to PW Botha.

With Zuma stubbornly clinging on and the Guptas showing no sense of shame or backing off, I felt that the entire nation was now in peril and not just Lady Justice as I had portrayed in this graphic way in the past. Once again, the response to the cartoon was huge outrage and plenty of support in equal measure.

I was very upset at having to include Gupta editor Moegsien Williams in this cartoon. He was someone with a rich history as a struggle journalist whom I had worked under on many publications since 1987. Somewhere along the line, he had seriously lost his bearings.

Zuma's succession was dominating discussion. He could not run again for president of the country in 2019. Technically he could stand again as party president at the Nasrec elective conference scheduled for December 2017. His priority clearly was protecting himself once he had left office. His ex-wife Nkosazana Dlamini-Zuma was back from running the African Union and was widely touted as a candidate.

At last, Cyril Ramaphosa stuck his head above the parapet. After serving as Zuma's party deputy for six rotten years, he entered the leadership fray, decrying corrupt patronage and demanding a judicial inquiry into State Capture.

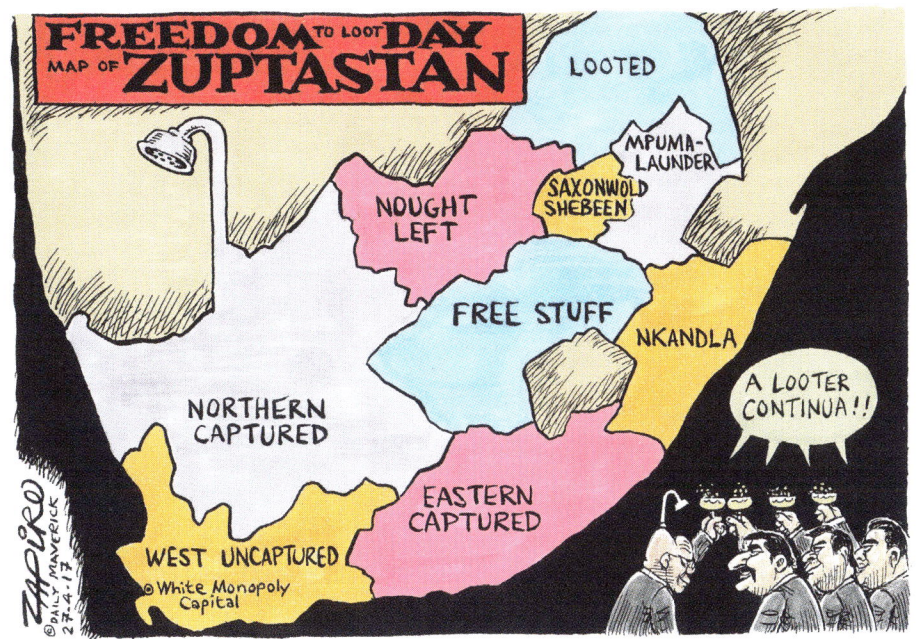

A distinctly uncelebratory Freedom Day 2017 was followed by a May Day Cosatu rally at which Zuma was booed and prevented from speaking.

Public enterprises minister Lynne Brown was very much in the State Capture spotlight. She was responsible for several major organisations which had clearly been subverted in the Guptas' interests. A well-respected activist and former premier of the Western Cape, Brown's compliance in this process was puzzling for me. She made many seriously compromised decisions and got herself into a real tangle trying to resolve Brian Molefe's fate — actually re-appointing him to Eskom to avoid the company paying him the R30m severance package.

My disillusionment with Brown was compounded by the memory of receiving from her, as a representative of my family, a commemorative plate to mark the renaming of the Claremont ANC branch as the Gaby Shapiro Branch, after my late mother.

Now just an ordinary MP, Pravin Gordhan crashed back into the Zuptas through some aggressive questioning during parliamentary committee hearings. He started with a roasting of the Eskom board and Lynne Brown. In the original cartoon, Gordhan was bursting into a parliamentary room. For the 2017 annual's cover I amended it to make a much wider point which some people thought was being premature. They believed that Zuma and the Guptas still held the upper hand and that Pravin's progress represented wishful thinking. But I felt strongly that we were moving in the right direction. I was really pleased that it was Pravin who was the main speaker at the launch of the annual.

I had joined *Daily Maverick* late in 2016 and felt right at home. We started having weekly breakfasts to kick around ideas and stories with my old friend Marianne Thamm and that Serbian force of nature, *DM* founder and editor Branko Brkic.

There were some conspiratorial whispers around *DM* that something big was happening and, suddenly, Branko was out of the country. I soon discovered what it was about. Branko had headed overseas to secure a stash of 200,000 Gupta e-mails which had been leaked to him from a computer that had gone in for repairs.

In June 2017 this all exploded into life as #GuptaLeaks, which changed the game. The treasure trove of documents exposed the monumental extent of State Capture. It also showed just how cavalier the Guptas had been in leaving a trail of damning e-mails.

In a rare joint media operation, *Daily Maverick* worked with, among others, the amaBhungane Centre for Investigative Journalism, which had been working on Gupta stories for seven years and now had all the corroboration they needed.

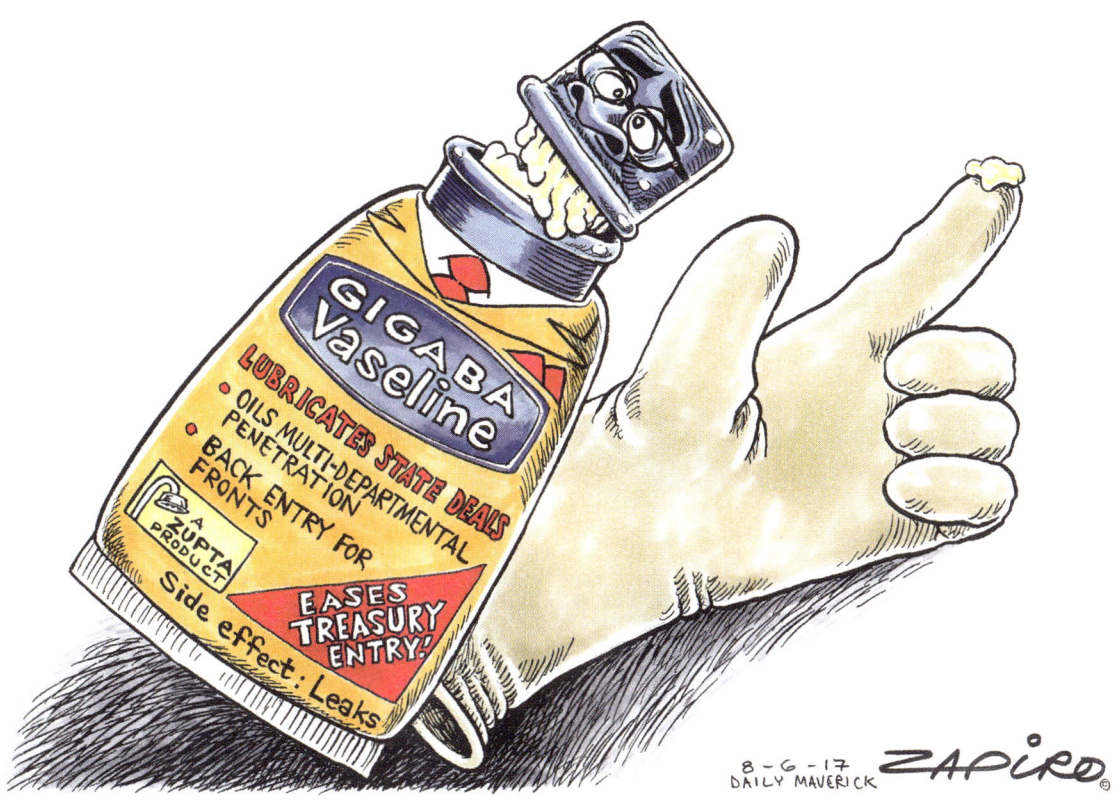

New finance minister Malusi Gigaba was named and shamed in the leaks — when he was public enterprises minister he had appointed several Gupta associates to key positions.

The Gupta Leaks also revealed that the taxpayer indirectly funded the extravagant and infamous Gupta family wedding at Sun City in 2013.

If Thuli Madonsela had still been around, she would have been pursuing the #GuptaLeaks revelations with gusto but her lame successor as public protector, Busisiwe Mkhwebane, ignored them and went after an apartheid-era bank payout instead with a report that went way beyond her powers and was later found to be unconstitutional.

NPA head Shaun Abrahams was also missing in action.

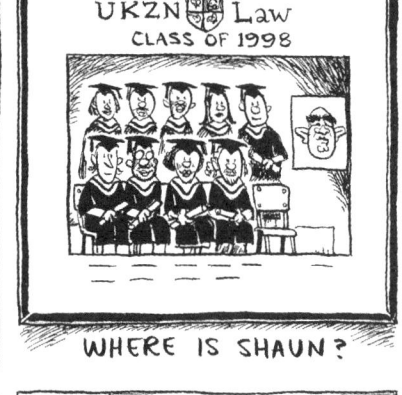

Abrahams made a self-justifying appearance in front of a parliamentary committee, claiming he was all action on State Capture and that there was an eight-legged investigation.

The Guptas were getting increasingly desperate. They mounted a social media smear campaign against their opponents, including the vicious targeting of journalists, that was traced to proxies operating so-called 'sockpuppet accounts' from their premises.

FEBRUARY 2017–DECEMBER 2017 | 223

We would later learn the true extent of this disinformation warfare, which was largely orchestrated by UK public relations firm Bell Pottinger. Thankfully they got their comeuppance when the massive reaction to this abuse of our democracy, and to the deliberate stirring up of racial tensions, caused the whole company to collapse.

Part of the sinister PR plan was to cynically play populist politics with land redistribution. The old 'Willing Buyer, Willing Seller' policy was being aggressively questioned, which was deeply ironic given what the Guptas had been able to get away with.

The GuptaLeaks revelations kept dragging more people and companies into the Zupta orbit. I worked like crazy to cram as many of the main players into this cartoon, with Brian Molefe as the barman in the shebeen. The next morning I got a congratulatory WhatsApp from my long-time lawyer Dario Milo which ended with "… but where's McKinsey?" I had included KPMG and German software maker SAP but had somehow left out the global consultants who were in it up to their necks through a deal with Gupta-linked Trillian Capital Partners.

In addition to their leaked e-mail woes, the Guptas found their taxes and contracts scrutinised and their bank accounts closed. I remember drawing this cartoon on a layout pad on a flight to Europe.

The continuing fallout gave me a chance to rectify my earlier omission of McKinsey from the roll call of guilty parties.

There was big advance talk of ANC action against Zuma at a policy conference but, as usual, it came to nothing.

The ANC also could not decide what to do about a motion of no confidence in Zuma in parliament. Opposition parties were demanding a secret ballot but speaker Baleka Mbete, famous for her signature elaborate headgear, resisted the call. Chief Justice Mogoeng Mogoeng ruled that a secret ballot was legal but not obligatory and that the speaker must decide on its use rationally and not favour her party. Mbete, to the surprise of many and to the anger of Zuma, did allow the secret ballot to proceed.

The secrecy of voting raised the genuine prospect that Zuma might lose his job.

There were some important defections in the ANC vote but he survived once again.

The Guptas continued to extricate themselves from their SA companies. They sold their media assets at inflated values to mouthpiece Mzwanele Manyi and they lent him the money for the deal.

SAA was a running sore throughout the Zuma years, haemorrhaging money as the fiefdom of chair Dudu Myeni. The new finance minister floated the idea of selling off a stake in Telkom to fund the airline.

The president's most captured son gave a very strange TV interview in Dubai.

A curious monument to Jacob Zuma was erected in Groot Marico in North West province at the behest of his acolyte, premier Supra Mahumapelo. It was situated where Zuma and more than 50 other Umkhonto weSizwe recruits had been arrested by the apartheid police in 1963 as they made their way to Botswana to undergo military training.

Without a hint of irony, the billboard marking the monument was headlined 'Jacob Zuma's Capture Site'.

After nine years of Stalingrad-like legal tactics, Zuma's lawyers admitted in the Supreme Court that the NPA's decision to drop 783 charges against him was irrational.

Alarm bells rang when Zuma announced yet another cabinet reshuffle in October 2017, this time without party approval.

The key move was that of his tame state security minister David Mahlobo to the energy portfolio, seemingly to ram through the nuclear deal with Russia, which was rumoured to potentially deliver huge payoffs for Zuma and his cronies.

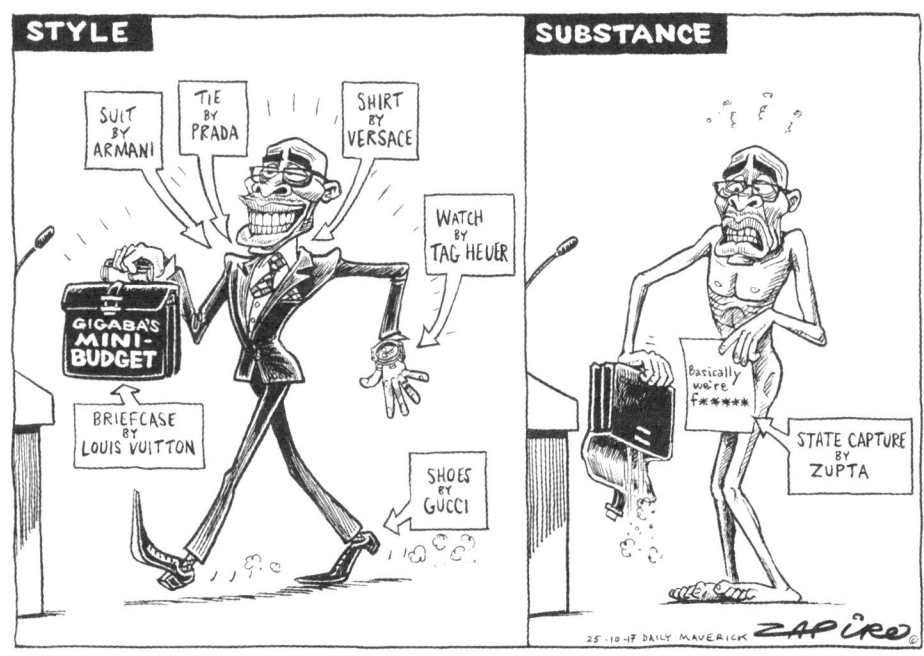

The local law enforcement agencies were not doing their jobs. They were too compromised to move against the Guptas. But, in America, the FBI and the Department of Justice had probes into the brothers under way, and, in the UK, the Financial Conduct Authority, the National Crime Agency and the Serious Fraud Office were looking into money laundering.

Malusi Gigaba, always long on looks and short on action, gave his 2017 mid-term policy statement.

Veteran investigative reporter Jacques Pauw's book *The President's Keepers* outlined the full extent of Zuma's shady empire. It hit a huge nerve and was snapped up in record numbers. And it sparked threats of legal action and verbal intimidation from intelligence agencies.

I drew these cartoons before I had fully read the book. If I had waited a bit longer, I would have put Arthur Fraser very prominently in the drawings. One of Jacques' biggest revelations for me was the sinister importance of Fraser's role at the State Security Agency.

Jacques Pauw's certainly wasn't the only book on the shelves about Zuma and the Guptas.

Khwezi came back to haunt Zuma when Redi Tlhabi wrote his rape accuser's life story.

In another rogue action, Zuma ignored the recommendations of the report he'd commissioned on student fees, having sat on it for months, and arbitrarily announced free university education. He didn't worry that the measure was unaffordable; he was simply trying to shore up his credentials just ahead of the ANC's elective conference.

In November 2017, Robert Mugabe, long propped up by the South African government, finally stepped down to widespread jubilation.

Another legal hammering for Zuma.

The Pretoria High Court ruled Shaun Abrahams's appointment as national director of public prosecutions invalid because his predecessor's departure, engineered by Zuma, had been unlawful. Since the president had a vested interest in cases being investigated by the NPA, the court ruled that his deputy Cyril Ramaphosa must make the new appointment.

The Nasrec ANC conference, which would decide between Ramaphosa and Dlamini-Zuma as the party's next leader, was beset by rumours of delegates, and even entire delegations, being bought off.

Ramaphosa won the narrowest of victories on 18 December 2017 but was hamstrung by the election of tainted rivals like David Mabuza, Ace Magashule and Jessie Duarte into senior leadership positions. Free State premier Magashule in particular was in the web of the Guptas — his son worked for them, there were multiple allegations of corrupt contracts and he continued to describe them as "good businesspeople".

There were reports of missing and wrongly disqualified votes which could have swung the conference outcomes.

END OF AN ERROR

JANUARY 2018 AND THE AFTERMATH

Ramaphosa might have been leader of the party, but becoming the leader of the country was no simple matter when the incumbent was wily, immoral and desperate. Zuma stubbornly refused to take the dignified way out and resign.

Even when he finally contemplated leaving office before his term expired, Zuma insisted on a long delay while he introduced Ramaphosa to his 'friends' in the BRICS countries.

The wheels of state were now turning against Zuma and his allies. The Asset Forfeiture Unit got preservation orders to freeze assets against 14 people and entities linked to Gupta deals.

And the Hawks were digging deep into the way the Guptas, with Ace Magashule's assistance, had milked millions out of a Free State dairy farm project.

There was some positive stuff happening except the man at the top was going nowhere slowly. Zuma kept delaying what seemed to be his inevitable departure. Because the stakes were so high, it felt interminable. One sticking point was SONA 2018. Who would deliver the annual showpiece speech?

Throughout the weekend before SONA, the story shifted daily and even hourly. SONA was then postponed ... an unprecedented move ... while the ANC tried to avoid the undoubted embarrassment of Zuma ever appearing in parliament again as the nation's leader.

In a much-delayed rambling, shambling, self-justifying televised speech, once again made late at night as was his habit, Zuma finally stepped down.

This cartoon received 800,000 Facebook views in 24 hours and seemed to catch the mood of the nation.

Ramaphosa took the reins amidst a burst of relief and optimism, and delivered a well-received State of the Nation Address. But he had a tough, entrenched legacy of corruption to deal with.

The movie *Black Panther* was hugely popular and I began depicting Cyril as RamaPanther ... wearing those McDonald's-issue socks and takkies he went walking in so publicly. It allowed me to depict him as semi-heroic.

JANUARY 2018 AND THE AFTERMATH

Gigaba stayed on in his finance ministry job long enough to give the 2018 budget before being shunted by Cyril back to home affairs, where he had come from. Nhlanhla Nene returned from the wilderness to restore discipline and integrity to the Treasury. There was much frustration that Ramaphosa had been unable to completely axe several rotten characters.

Appearing before a parliamentary committee delving into his patent links with the Guptas, the usually cocky Gigaba cut a pathetic figure.

Even Shaun Abrahams, who was still in his job pending an appeal against the court ruling that his appointment was invalid, found some teeth. In March 2018, he announced that Zuma would go on trial in Durban for 16 charges, involving 783 incidents, of racketeering, corruption, money laundering and fraud. Now he said: "I am of the view that there are reasonable prospects of a successful prosecution of Zuma in the charges listed in the indictment." What had changed except the political leadership?

Predictably Zuma wasn't going down without a messy fight. He darkly threatened to reveal all about those who called him corrupt. He started rallying KZN and ethnic allies, and appearing at party events to portray himself as a victim of conspiracies and plots. "I've never committed any crime ... there's no criminal in my family," he said. He was hoping that a long game could see his allies block Ramaphosa in party committees and then overturn him at the next elective conference in 2022. Or maybe, some hinted, Zuma might form his own party .... something he denied. But who could ever trust a Zuma denial any more?

Despite his rumblings Zuma was now yesterday's man – even as he became a father yet again at the age of 76 with a new 24-year-old fiancée. Without his grubby hands on the levers of power, he was a discredited and desperate figure. Somehow it seemed a fitting political epitaph that I should put him on the cover of Big Issue magazine covered in poo.